I
Can
Problem
Solve

KINDERGARTEN
&
PRIMARY GRADES

D1533278

An Interpersonal Cognitive Problem-Solving Program

Myrna B. Shure

Research Press   2612 North Mattis Avenue   Champaign Illinois 61821

Illustrations 1–49, the feeling face drawings (in Lesson 30), the ICPS
Teacher Self-Evaluation Checklist (in Appendix A), the ICPS Dialoguing
Reminders (Appendix B), and the ICPS Word Concept Illustrations
(Appendix C) in this volume may be copied for noncommercial classroom
use only. No other part of this book may be reproduced by any means
without the written permission of the publisher. Excerpts may be printed
in connection with published reviews in periodicals without express
permission.

Copies of this book may be ordered from the publisher at the address
given on the title page.

Illustrations by Joseph Mingroni, William Renn, and Herbert Wimble
Cover design and illustration by Doug Burnett
Composition by Wadley Graphix Corporation

ISBN 0–87822–339–8
Library of Congress Catalog No. 92–81468

This program is dedicated to George Spivack,
my friend and research collaborator of 25 years.

CONTENTS

PRE-PROBLEM-SOLVING SKILLS

PROBLEM-SOLVING SKILLS

Alternative Solutions   225

Consequences   269

LIST OF COMPLEMENTARY APPLICATIONS

ACKNOWLEDGMENTS

This program was developed as part of a larger research project funded by NIMH grants #MH20372 (1971–1975) and #MH40801 (1987–1992), Washington, DC, and conducted in cooperation with Dr. Irvin J. Farber, Director of Research, School District of Philadelphia. I wish to convey my gratitude to Dr. Constance E. Clayton, Superintendent, and Leontine D. Scott, Associate Superintendent of School Operations, School District of Philadelphia, for their support of ICPS in the schools throughout the years. Appreciation goes to Dr. Milton Goldberg, then Executive Director of Early Childhood Programs, and Frances Becker, then Director of Education of Young Children, who paved the way for the first research efforts in 1971. These early efforts were the cornerstone for the curriculum conducted in the Philadelphia schools at the present time.

Special thanks go to George Spivack, whose initial research with adolescents demonstrated a clear association between interpersonal cognitive problem-solving skills and behavior. His vision—that enhancing interpersonal thinking skills could reduce or prevent high-risk behaviors—inspired the creation of day-by-day lesson-games to reach those goals. George's help and guidance were instrumental in identifying age-appropriate skills and paved the way for the present program for the kindergarten and primary grades.

A very special thank you to everyone at Research Press, particularly to Ann Wendel, President, Russell Pence, Vice President of Marketing, and Dennis Wiziecki, Advertising Manager, for their belief in and enthusiasm for ICPS programming in the schools; to Suzanne Wagner, for her design of the pages, which makes them pleasing to look at and easy to read; and to my editor, Karen Steiner, who in her own inimitable style of ICPS let me know that "There's more than one way" to express a thought. Karen's careful attention to the littlest details and her patience with my never-ending questions made me feel safe and secure.

Recognition and appreciation go to the many Philadelphia teachers who conducted the program with their kindergarten classes during its original research phase and to their principals, who offered their continued cooperation and support:

Hill Elementary School: Oscar Goss, principal, Gwendolyn Peyton and Carole Williams, teachers

Huey Elementary School: Dr. Donald Rouse, principal, Ruth Holland and Doris Schoener, teachers

Leidy Elementary School: Bernard Belasco, principal, Christine Haliburton and Judith Wachstein, teachers

Locke Elementary School: Dr. James Barksdale, principal, Betty Hill, teacher

Meade Elementary School: Mark Levin, principal, Jamesena Carrington and Barbara Wiley, team members, and Frances Howell, teacher

Rhoads Elementary School: Dr. Robert Chapman, principal, June Crawford and Francine Rice, teachers

Special recognition and appreciation go to more Philadelphia teachers and principals who participated in the subsequent research phase:

Blankenburg Elementary School: Dr. Agnes Barksdale, principal, May Berger, Elaine French, and Gloria Reid, kindergarten teachers, Connie Kennedy, first-grade teacher

W. D. Kelley Elementary School: Anthony Bellos, principal, Varnelle Moore, kindergarten teacher

Locke Elementary School: Dr. James Barksdale, principal, Robin Cooper, Trudy Dolgin, and Mary Lewis, kindergarten teachers

Martha Washington Elementary School: Dr. Harold Trawick, principal, Norma Brunson, Gita Farbman, and Mercedes Sadler, kindergarten teachers

McDaniel Elementary School: Carolyn Garvin, principal, Bonnie Koval, Ethel Mincey, and Helene Zeitzer, kindergarten teachers, Linda Braun and Mary Marincola, first-grade teachers

Robert Morris Elementary School: James Jones, principal, Judy Charles and Kate Ellis, kindergarten teachers, Rose Keane and Rita Williams, first-grade teachers

Appreciation also goes to Janet Samuels, who, in becoming principal of the Locke School upon Dr. James Barksdale's retirement, became an important addition to our team, as did Christine Lindsey, who became principal of Martha Washington, and Marshall Gorodetzer, who became principal of Robert Morris during ICPS research at those schools.

Gratitude is expressed to Phyllis Ditlow and Virginia Jamison, ICPS coordinators for the Philadelphia Public Schools' School Age Programs, directed by James W. Gaskins. They have implemented the program as part of service funded by the Pew Charitable Trust (1983–1986) and have contributed greatly to the present revision, both in the presentation of ICPS concepts and in the integration of these concepts into the standardized curriculum. To participating research teachers Judy Charles, Kate Ellis, and Rose Keane, for their consultation leading to further revisions after completion of the program, I am also deeply grateful.

Thanks are also due Joan Algeo and Kathleen Shea, my own research assistants, who developed some of the revised lessons and who brought added joy to the children through their enterprising use of puppets, role-plays, and problem-solving dialogues.

Redesign of the ICPS lessons has also benefited from conversations and contributions from others who have creatively adapted the program for use in their own cities, particularly Bonnie Aberson, school psychologist and ICPS project coordinator; Charlie Albury, Susan Gutting, Frances Mann, and Barbara Trushin of the Dade County, Florida, Public Schools; and Eileen Altman of the Mental Health Association in Illinois (MHAI), together with Judy Rappin, a teacher in the Chicago public schools.

Spearheaded by the MHAI, a larger, more systematic implementation of the ICPS curriculum was undertaken in the Chicago public schools. Thanks are due Laura M. Caravello, Prevention Coordinator for MHAI; Paul A. Downing, Vice President of Labor Relations, Ameritech Services, Inc.; Dr. Edith Fifer, Administrator for Early Childhood Special Education Programs, Chicago Public Schools; Jan Holcomb, Executive Director of MHAI; Dr. James G. Kelly, professor of psychology at the University of Illinois at Chicago and Project Consultant for MHAI; and Ann Nerad, Project Founder and former MHAI board president and member.

Recognition also goes to the Chicago pilot expansion schools for pioneering the ICPS program in their city:

Alexandre Dumas School: Silvia L. Peters, principal

Keller Gifted Magnet School: Ruth Muth, principal

Pilsen Community Academy: William Levin, principal

William Claude Reavis Elementary School: Dr. Winifred French, principal

Franz Schubert Elementary School: Dr. Cynthia A. Wnek, principal

George B. Swift Elementary School: Dr. Seymour Miller, principal

Carter G. Woodson South Elementary School: John F. Hawkins, principal

The staff of these schools—40 teachers and teacher assistants in regular, bilingual, and special education classes from kindergarten through second grade—found unique ways to use the ICPS curriculum. I am thrilled that ICPS is flourishing in the city where I grew up and is being used in the George B. Swift Elementary School, where I spent my own childhood from kindergarten through eighth grade. To hear a 5-year-old say, "I Can Problem Solve" in the very school in which I was a 5-year-old is especially touching.

INTRODUCTION

Every day, some kind of interpersonal problem arises between children, a child and a teacher, or a child and other authority figures. Some children can cope with and solve these kinds of problems very well; others appear less able to think them through. Over 20 years of research has shown that, as early as age 4, children can learn that behavior has causes, that people have feelings, and that there is more than one way to solve a problem. They can also decide whether an idea is or is not a good one.

This volume, along with two companion volumes designed for preschool and intermediate elementary grades, shows teachers how to help children learn to solve the problems they have with others.* The approach is the same for all three volumes. Although some of the most popular lessons are repeated here from the preschool book, most lessons are either more sophisticated or completely new. They are designed to be adapted for various levels of ability throughout the early primary grades. Although the formal research on the present program has been done with kindergarten and first-grade children, project coordinators in the Philadelphia public schools have used this material successfully with some children through the third grade, in regular as well as in transition and special education classes.

The approach employed, originally called Interpersonal Cognitive Problem Solving, has come to be called I Can Problem Solve (ICPS) by the many adults and children who have used it. Although children with serious emotional disturbances will likely require more individual attention and/or outside professional help, ICPS offers a practical approach to help most children learn to evaluate and deal with problems. Its underlying goal is to help children learn *how* to think, not *what* to think. It does not tell them what to do when conflict or other problem situations come up. Rather, it gives children ways to talk about their view of problems and think problems through. The main goal, focus, content, method, and benefits of ICPS are summarized on the following page.

As this summary suggests, the benefits of ICPS training are numerous. Research has shown that when children learn to use problem-solving thinking, their social adjustment improves, with significant reductions in nagging and demanding, emotional upset, and social withdrawal. Children become more able to wait, share, and take turns, as well as to get along with others.

---

* The other volumes in the program, *I Can Problem Solve: An Interpersonal Cognitive Problem-Solving Program (Preschool)* and *I Can Problem Solve: An Interpersonal Cognitive Problem-Solving Program (Intermediate Elementary Grades)*, are also available from Research Press. For information about immediate and long-term scientific research findings, as well as about measures of alternative solution skills and consequential thinking skills, contact Dr. Myrna Shure, Hahnemann University, Broad & Vine MS–626, Philadelphia, PA 19102.

THE ICPS PROGRAM

GOAL To teach children thinking skills that can be used to help resolve or prevent "people" problems

FOCUS Teaches children *how* to think, not *what* to think
Guides children to think for themselves
Teaches children how to evaluate their own ideas
Encourages children to come up with many solutions to problems on their own

CONTENT **Pre-Problem-Solving Skills**
Learning a problem-solving vocabulary
Identifying one's own and others' feelings
Considering other people's points of view
Learning sequencing and timing of events

Problem-Solving Skills
Thinking of more than one solution
Considering consequences
Deciding which solution to choose

METHOD Teaches skills through the use of games, stories, puppets, and role-playing
Guides the use of skills in real-life situations
Integrates ideas into standard curriculum

BENEFITS **For Children**
Fun for children—presents lessons in game form
Builds self-confidence
Builds listening skills
Encourages generation of alternative solutions
Provides skills to handle new problems
Facilitates social interaction among peers
Teaches skills applicable to other situations
Increases sensitivity to others, sharing, and caring
Increases independence
Increases ability to wait
Increases ability to cope with frustration
Decreases impulsivity
Decreases social withdrawal

For Teachers
Reinforces other curriculum goals
Creates a more positive classroom atmosphere
Decreases time spent handling conflicts
Enhances teachers' own problem-solving skills
Deepens insight into children's thoughts and feelings

Regardless of temperament, children become better liked and more aware of—even genuinely concerned about—the feelings of others. In brief, children who have learned the ICPS concepts are more successful in getting what they want when they can have it and are better able to cope with frustration when they cannot. Finally, ICPS not only helps lessen problem behaviors, but 1- and 2-year follow-up studies, and our recent 5-year longitudinal study (1987–1992), suggest that it can actually prevent their occurrence.

Evidence that the program is having an impact becomes noticeable to the teacher as children begin to use the language of problem solving in the classroom. During the early weeks, most children will begin to adopt the initial verbal concept skills outside of formal training, although it is not until later in the program that children begin to solve interpersonal problems on their own.

Some inhibited children will begin to speak up after only 2 or 3 weeks of the program, and many start relating to others by the end of the first 2 months. Changes in impulsive behavior take somewhat longer to occur, but most children show signs of increased patience, reduced emotionality, and readiness to talk things over before the final lesson is conducted.

As they learn the ICPS skills and how to use them, academic test scores improve, and impulsive youngsters become less aggressive, less emotional in the face of frustration, and less impatient. Inhibited youngsters become less withdrawn and better able to stand up for their rights. At program's end, some youngsters may still act aggressively or impulsively, but they will have begun to talk about what they do in a way that indicates overt behavior change will soon follow. Although it takes time for such major behavior changes to occur, teachers find that helping children learn to think for themselves is well worth the effort.

PROGRAM OVERVIEW

The ICPS program for kindergarten and primary grades includes both formal lessons and specific suggestions for incorporating ICPS principles in classroom interactions and the curriculum.

ICPS Lesson Content

Each of the 83 ICPS lessons contains a stated purpose, list of suggested materials, and a teacher script. The teacher script, intended as a flexible guideline, explains the basic steps in conducting the lesson.

As the outline on the following page shows, the lessons are grouped into two major categories: pre-problem-solving skills and problem-solving skills. The ICPS words and other pre-problem-solving concepts set the stage for the problem-solving skills, which are associated with alternative solutions, consequences, and solution-consequence pairs. If children have experienced the preschool ICPS program, they may already be familiar with some of the earlier concepts. However, because the lessons build toward specific goals in problem-solving thinking, it is important to conduct each one.

The vocabulary taught in the pre-problem-solving phase of the program plays a critical role in later problem-solving thinking. In the lessons, as in

OUTLINE OF ICPS LESSONS

LESSONS	PURPOSE
	Pre-Problem-Solving Skills
1–14	To teach the following ICPS word concepts: IS-NOT, OR-AND, SOME-ALL, IF-THEN, SAME-DIFFERENT, BEFORE-AFTER, and NOW-LATER
15–19	To help children learn to identify their own and others' feelings of being HAPPY, SAD, and ANGRY, as well as to introduce the word concepts MIGHT-MAYBE (to help children avoid quick and faulty assumptions about others)
20–21	To encourage skills associated with listening and paying attention
22–26	To help children learn ways to find out about others' preferences, to reinforce the word concepts MIGHT-MAYBE, and to introduce the concepts WHY-BECAUSE (to help children begin to become aware that behavior and feelings have causes)
27–39	To identify and express feelings of being AFRAID, PROUD, and FRUSTRATED, as well as to teach attention to the sequencing of events and when a time to do something IS or is NOT a good one
40–42	To help children understand what is FAIR and NOT FAIR in light of the rights of others and to illustrate that fairness sometimes means having to wait
43–45	To teach the meaning of the word IMPATIENT, strengthen awareness of sequencing, and help children cope with frustration when they must wait for something
46–47	To convey the concepts WORRIED-RELIEVED and further encourage sensitivity to children's own and others' feelings
	Problem-Solving Skills
48–60	**Alternative solutions:** To help children recognize what a problem is and learn ways to generate many possible solutions
61–74	**Consequences:** To help children learn to think sequentially as a prerequisite to understanding cause-and-effect relationships (Lessons 61–67) and to encourage actual consequential thinking (Lessons 68–74)
75–83	**Solution-consequence pairs:** To give children practice in linking a solution with a possible consequence in a one-to-one fashion

the following paragraphs, these words are capitalized to suggest the emphasis they should be given. First, the words IS and NOT help children later think, "This IS a good idea; that is NOT." Subsequently, children learn the meanings of the words SAME and DIFFERENT. These words help children understand, for instance, that hitting and kicking are kind of the SAME because they both involve hurting someone. Children can also begin to think, "I can think of something DIFFERENT to do." Other lessons help children identify their own and others' feelings, understand that there is more than one way to find out how someone feels (by watching, listening, or asking), and comprehend that DIFFERENT people may feel DIFFERENT ways about the SAME thing.

The basic ICPS word concepts not only help children recognize and find out about others' feelings, they suggest ways these feelings may be influenced. Considering people's preferences is one of these ways. Young children often assume others like the SAME things they do (often leading to faulty conclusions and, therefore, unsuccessful solutions). Through the lessons, children come to appreciate that if one way to make someone feel HAPPY is not successful, it is possible to try a DIFFERENT way.

As a precursor to consequential thinking, a lesson on the words WHY and BECAUSE helps children appreciate the impact of what they do on themselves and others. This understanding will help them later on to think, for instance, "He hit me BECAUSE I took his toy." Inasmuch as the effects of one's actions on another are never a certainty, the words MIGHT and MAYBE are introduced. Building up to the final problem-solving skills, other lessons concern what people like and how people feel when deciding how to solve an interpersonal problem, the sequencing of events and whether an idea IS or is NOT a good one BECAUSE of what MIGHT happen next, and the notion that there are lots of DIFFERENT ways to solve the SAME problem.

Conducting ICPS Lessons

Teachers have found the following suggestions for conducting ICPS lessons helpful with children at the kindergarten and primary levels:

1. Present the lessons to the children as "games" in which they have a chance to learn and practice new skills. You may wish to spend no more than 15 to 20 minutes a day on initial lessons, slowly increasing the length of sessions to about 30 minutes. This helps children adjust to the program and gradually increase their attention span.

2. Vary the wording of the teacher script to suit your group. Creativity with the content is encouraged as long as the concepts to be taught are not lost. It is not necessary to memorize the script. You may wish to place it on your lap, on the floor, or on a table and casually read from it. Once you get comfortable with the ICPS style of eliciting responses, you may be able to get along without the script at all.

3. It is possible to conduct ICPS lessons with an entire class of 30 or so children in one group. However, for heightened participation per child, smaller groups are preferable. Daily 20- to 40-minute lessons will take about 4 months to complete. If necessary, half

the class could be given ICPS lessons every other day, an option that still provides ample time to complete the program within the school year.

4. Because the program involves a good deal of child response, each group should have some quiet and some talkative children. A whole group of nonresponders would likely result in group silence.

5. It is best to avoid positioning the group near toys, bookshelves, or other potentially distracting objects. Two particularly disruptive children who are friends should be placed in separate groups. Specific techniques for handling "difficult" children are included in the lessons themselves, as well as in Appendix D in this volume.

6. Children can sit in chairs or on the floor, but a semicircle is preferable to a straight line. Older children may sit at their desks. Quieter or more inhibited youngsters should sit in front or near a teacher aide.

7. A teacher aide can assist in a number of ways. He or she can participate in the lesson and help by keeping the more disruptive children nearby to maintain interest and by occasionally encouraging the more inhibited youngsters to whisper a response. If the lessons are being conducted in small groups, the aide may need to stay with the other children in the class during the period of formal training. Alternatively, the aide can train a second group at the same time. Even if the aide does not participate in the formal lessons, he or she can apply the concepts during the day when real problems arise. A consistent approach by teacher and aide will help the children apply their learning.

8. The group does not need to be sitting quietly "at attention" before a lesson begins. If you begin the lesson with a fast, exciting pace, the children generally settle down and participate.

9. If your class is having problems in grasping a particular concept, this need not be a stumbling block. The program includes ample repetition of specific concepts, and most children will eventually learn them. For this reason, a child who misses a day or two of training need not be "caught up" individually. Some lessons (for example, Lessons 34, 43, and 46, which teach the feeling word concepts FRUSTRATED, IMPATIENT, and WORRIED-RELIEVED, may be too advanced for some kindergartners. If so, omit those lessons for your class.

10. If the group becomes restless early in a session, try an earlier lesson or a game such as Simon Says. If the group remains restless after returning to the lesson, stop for the day.

11. Go at the pace of your group. Many of the lessons are designed for various levels of learning ability. In Lesson 24, for example, children can be asked to remember as few as 3 or as many as 8 things at once. If your kindergartners or first graders are already

familiar with the word concepts of the early lessons, move through them quickly *but do not skip them.* Each concept plays a role in the sequence and is needed as a frame of reference in later, more sophisticated lessons. Many youngsters know words such as NOT, AND, OR, and so forth, but they may not actually think in terms of negation (NOT), multiples (AND), or alternatives (OR). You may begin with Lesson 15 for children at the upper-primary level.

12. In some lessons, expect a high level of verbal participation. The goal is to encourage problem-solving thinking, and this goal is reflected in ideas being expressed openly.

13. Lessons are designed to help the inhibited child participate via body motions, pointing, and so forth. The extremely nonverbal child should be encouraged to participate in these motions but should not be pushed, at least initially, to verbalize.

14. You may refer to situations illustrated or offered by children as *problems.* The children come to understand this word—as one youngster was heard to reveal proudly, "I solved a problem today!"

15. In addition to using the problems presented, children can make up problems or describe situations that really happened to them. The class can then offer solutions or consequences, elicited with the same techniques designed for the problem situations provided in the lessons.

16. Role-playing can be especially useful if children are able to act out the various parts in the problem situations. If the children in your class are capable of role-playing beyond that suggested by the situations included in the lessons, encourage such activity to maintain interest.

Complementary Applications

Helping children associate how they think with what they do in real-life situations is essential to the success of the program. As noted previously, suggestions are made periodically throughout the book for applying ICPS skills in the classroom—both in interpersonal situations that may arise during the day and in the curriculum. Suggestions for interaction in the classroom and integration in the curriculum are given after the lesson or group of lessons to which they pertain. Presented on bordered pages, these complementary applications are just as important as the formal lessons.

Illustrations and Other Program Materials

The ICPS lessons make use of a number of illustrations, which immediately follow the lessons to which they pertain. You may choose to copy or even enlarge these illustrations and display them so children can see and point to them easily during the lesson, or you may place the illustrations under an opaque projector. Yet another alternative is to duplicate the illustrations and have children color and display them in the classroom to help reinforce the skills taught.

Other suggested materials are readily available in the classroom: chalkboard or easel, animal or people hand puppets, miscellaneous classroom objects (for example, crayons or blocks), and age-appropriate storybooks. In the case of hand puppets, any available can be substituted for those depicted in the lessons.

Some lessons involve the use of "feeling faces" showing the emotions HAPPY, SAD, ANGRY, and AFRAID. Children may draw these faces, or you and/or the children may copy the feeling faces provided in Lesson 30 and, using double-stick tape, make feeling face stickers. If you choose to make the stickers, you will need approximately 6 of each of the faces (a total of 24) for each child to use during the program.

Appendix Content

Four appendixes complete this volume. Appendix A offers some guidelines for continued ICPS teaching once the formal lessons have been completed. Some questions are included to help teachers think about how they communicate key ICPS concepts to children. This appendix also includes the ICPS Teacher Self-Evaluation Checklist, intended to help teachers gauge their ability to use ICPS teaching on an ongoing basis.

Appendix B offers a summary of the steps and questions teachers ask in dialoguing child-child and teacher-child problems. These pages can be duplicated and posted in the classroom to help teachers remember how to use the ICPS approach when everyday problems arise.

Appendix C provides supplementary illustrations depicting ICPS word concepts. These illustrations may be displayed on bulletin boards within the children's reach or used as flash cards. If this is done, children can play "teacher" by pointing to an illustration and asking another student to make up a sentence using the word. These illustrations also serve to remind teachers to use ICPS words on a daily basis.

Appendix D summarizes techniques the teacher can use in the formal lessons to deal with shy, nonresponsive; disruptive or obstinate; dominating; and silly behaviors.

ICPS DIALOGUING

Central to the ICPS program is the process of problem-solving dialoguing. In ICPS dialoguing, the teacher guides the child in applying ICPS concepts to solve a real-life problem. This type of dialoguing reflects a style of thought that will help children try again if their first attempt to solve a problem should fail and learn to cope with frustration when their desires must be delayed or denied.

The program contains many examples of dialoguing. Even very early in the program, the teacher may conduct what are called "mini-dialogues" with children. After Lessons 1 through 68 have been completed, the children will be ready for full ICPS dialogues in which they identify a problem, generate alternative solutions, explore consequences, and choose the best solution.

ICPS Dialoguing Procedures

The nature of the problem that arises will determine the exact procedures for ICPS dialoguing. In general, you will want to try to help children identify the problem, appreciate their own and others' feelings, think of solutions to the problem, and anticipate the consequences of a solution.

You will not need to memorize a set of specific questions. However, the following steps in dialoguing child-child problems and questions for resolving teacher-child conflicts will give you a sense of what is involved.

Child-child problems

STEP 1: Define the problem.

What happened? What's the matter?

That will help me understand the problem better.

STEP 2: Elicit feelings.

How do you feel?

How does _____ feel?

STEP 3: Elicit consequences.

What happened when you did that?

STEP 4: Elicit feelings about consequences.

How did you feel when _____?
(*For example:* He took your toy/she hit you)

STEP 5: Encourage the child to think of alternative solutions.

Can you think of a DIFFERENT way to solve this
problem so _____?
(*For example:* You both won't be mad/she won't hit you)

STEP 6: Encourage evaluation of the solution.

Is that a good idea or NOT a good idea?

If a good idea: Go ahead and try that.

If not a good idea: Oh, you'll have to think of something DIFFERENT.

STEP 7: Praise the child's act of thinking.

If the solution works: Oh, you thought of that all by yourself. You're a good problem solver!

If the solution does not work: Oh, you'll have to think of something DIFFERENT. I know you're a good thinker!

Teacher-child problems

Can I talk to you AND to _____ at the SAME time?

Is that a good place to _____?
(*For example:* Draw/leave your food)

Can you think of a good place to _____?

Is this a good time to _____?
(*For example:* Talk to your neighbor/talk to me)

When IS a good time?

How do you think I feel when you _____?
(*For example:* Don't listen/throw food/interrupt me)

Can you think of something DIFFERENT to do until _____?
(*For example:* You can fingerpaint/I can get what you want/I can help you)

Once children become accustomed to ICPS dialoguing, most can respond to a considerably shortened version of questioning. For instance, just asking, "Can you think of a DIFFERENT idea?" is often enough to cue children that they need to apply their problem-solving skills.

Basic Principles of ICPS Dialoguing

Five basic principles, applicable to children as young as age 4, underlie the dialoguing process. The only prerequisite is that children understand the basic word concepts used by the adult. Relatively consistent application of these principles in time helps children associate their newly acquired thinking skills with what they do and how they behave.

First, both child and teacher must identify the problem. Casually saying, "What happened?"; "What's the matter?"; or "Tell me about it" not only helps the child clarify the problem but also ensures that you will not jump to a faulty conclusion about what is going on. For example: "Oh, now I see what the *problem* is. I thought you were mad because your friend took your book. Now I see it's because she had it too long and won't give it back." Discovering the child's view of the problem starts the dialoguing process on the proper course.

Second, when dialoguing, it is important to understand and deal with the real problem. The child in the preceding example thinks he has already shared his book with his friend, but the teacher may see this child grab the book and erroneously assume that grabbing is the problem. Actually, grabbing is the child's *solution* to the problem of getting his book back, not the problem itself. From the child's point of view, the real problem is that he wants his book back.

Third, once the real problem has been identified, the teacher must not alter it to fit his or her own needs. Suppose that the teacher becomes intent on showing the child in the example how to share his things. Because the child is thinking only about how to get back something he knows he has already shared, the teacher's guidance will likely lead to resistance. In this case, attempting to teach the "right" thing to do may backfire.

Fourth, the child, not the teacher, must solve the problem. If the child is to develop the habit of thinking of his own solutions to problems and considering the potential consequences of his actions, he must be encouraged to think for himself. More than simply "listening" to the child, the teacher must actively draw out what the child thinks caused the problem, how he and others feel about the situation, his ideas about how to solve the difficulty, and what he thinks might happen if he were to put those ideas into action. In highlighting the child's thinking, the teacher does not offer solutions to the problem or suggest what might happen next. When not bombarded with "don'ts" or offered a stream of suggestions about "do's," the child is freed to think through the problem and decide for himself what and what not to do. The teacher only asks questions and, through these, guides and encourages the emergence of problem-solving thinking.

Finally, the focus is on how *the child thinks, not on* what *he thinks (in other words, the specific conclusions he comes to).* Research on the ICPS program suggests that the process of a child's thinking is more important in the long run than the content of a specific solution. Attention is therefore focused on developing a style of thinking that will help the child deal with interpersonal problems in general, not on solving the immediate problem to the teacher's satisfaction (although this often occurs). Praising a solution may inhibit further thought about other ideas. Criticizing a solution may inhibit the child's speaking freely about what is on his mind. In either case, the child's thinking will shift from generating options, consequences, and causes to selecting the one thing that meets with teacher approval. In applying these principles, the teacher transmits to the child the value judgment that *thinking* is important, and the child learns that thinking meets with adult approval.

When Not to Dialogue

It is not possible or even necessary to dialogue every problem that comes up. In fact, there are times when dialoguing is not effective and its use is better postponed. Clearly, if a child has been or is likely to be physically harmed, your first priority is to help by removing the child from danger.

In addition, sometimes a crying child just needs to cry—an angry child just needs to be angry. For example, Shelly, a super problem solver and socially competent child, was really bawling one day while fighting with LaTanya over some clay. When asked what was wrong, Shelly replied, "She (LaTanya) never shares. I always share with her!" The teacher did not dialogue with Shelly at this time. She recognized that Shelly was justifiably upset and would be able to problem solve by herself when she calmed down. In fact, she did just that.

Finally, just because your goal is to dialogue problem situations, this does not mean that you must never become angry yourself. Although angry displays should of course not be the predominant way in which you solve problems with or between children, anger is an emotion with which children must learn to cope, and your showing it occasionally is natural.

PRE-PROBLEM-SOLVING SKILLS

Teacher Script

If the group has had no previous experience with ICPS, use Version 1. If some or all of the children have ICPS training in an earlier grade, use Version 2.

Version 1

Each day, for a little while, we're going to play some games called ICPS. For us, this means I Can Problem Solve. *(Write these words on chalkboard or easel.)* We're going to start with games that have words in them that will help you solve problems. In some games we'll talk about how you and others feel about things. You know, things that make people feel happy, sad, or angry. Then we'll think of all the things children can do when they have a problem, like when they want someone to do something, or when someone is mad about something, or when people have to wait for what they want.

Some of you are already really good at this. But all of us can get even better. And children who can solve problems can feel proud to say, "I'm an ICPS kid because I Can Problem Solve."

You'll get the idea of the games as we go along. Today we're going to play a game about the words IS and NOT. Are you ready?

Proceed to Lesson 1 or to Lesson 15, depending on the level of your class.

Version 2

Some of you may have played some games before from a program called ICPS. Who can remember what the letters *ICPS* mean?

Let children respond, prompting as needed. Write "I Can Problem Solve" on chalkboard or easel.

Who can tell us some kinds of problems that ICPS helps to solve?

Let children respond, then summarize.

OK, ICPS is about problems that come up between people—other kids, or parents, or teachers, or any people. All of us at times have these kinds of problems, and some of them are harder to solve than others. No matter how good we are at this, we can all get even better, right?

We're going to be playing some more ICPS games now. You may have played some of them before, but most of them will be different or harder. If you didn't have this program before, it's OK. You'll get the idea of the activities as we go along. And those of you who did this before can help the rest of us. Let's start. Are you ready?

Proceed to Lesson 1 or to Lesson 15, depending on the level of your class.

Is-Not

PURPOSE

To present these word concepts so that children will later be able to decide whether an idea IS or is NOT a good one

MATERIALS

None

TEACHER SCRIPT

> **NOTE**
>
> Appendix C provides illustrations of this and other ICPS word concepts. These illustrations may be displayed on bulletin boards within the children's reach or used as flash cards. You may wish to begin with Lesson 15 for children at the upper-primary level.

Today's ICPS game is about the words IS and NOT. Ready?

My name IS _____. My name is NOT _____.

(To Child 1) Your name IS _____. Your name is NOT _____.

(To Child 2) Your name IS Rudolph.

Oh, you caught me. Your name IS _____.

(To the group) I am pointing to a book. I am NOT pointing to a _____.

What else is this NOT?

Let three or four children answer, then continue with the following questions. Have fun with the concept.

(To the group, if sunny outside) It IS raining outside.

Oh, it's NOT? I tried to trick you.

It is NOT raining. It IS _____.

(To Child 3) (Child 1) IS a girl. (Child 1) is NOT a _____. What else is (Child 1) NOT?

You can be silly: (Child 1) is NOT a balloon.

Let's think of lots of other things (Child 1) is NOT.

(Child 4), come up here. Point to something in the room or go and touch it.

(To the group) (He/she) IS pointing to a _____.

(He/she) is NOT pointing to a _____.

What else is (he/she) NOT pointing to?

Repeat as time and interest permit.

HINT

Emphasize the ICPS words shown in capital letters with your voice in this and other lessons.

ICPS Words: Is-Not

Try incorporating and building upon individual ICPS words as they are presented. This will help you later on when you apply ICPS dialogues with children and will help the children extend learning to real life.

JUICETIME/LUNCHTIME

This IS (for example, juice). It is NOT _____.

This IS a (hamburger). It is NOT a _____.

This (potato) IS (yellow). It is NOT _____.

I am your teacher. I am NOT a _____.

(Child 1) IS a (boy/girl). (He/she) is NOT a monkey.

What else is (he/she) NOT?

LINING UP

This IS the boys' line. It is NOT the _____.

IS the boys' line longer than the girls' line?

(Yes/no), it (IS/is NOT) longer than the girls' line.

We are ready to go to (gym). We are NOT going to _____.

FREE PLAY

What IS (Child 1) doing?

What is (Child 2) NOT doing?

Who IS wearing a (white top)?

Who is NOT wearing a (blue top)?

(About a child who is not painting) _____ IS painting.

(He/she) is NOT?

Oh, I tried to trick you. What IS (he/she) doing?

This IS a (crayon). It is NOT a _____.

This IS a (desk). It is NOT a _____.

LISTENING AND PARTICIPATING

(Child 1) IS listening.

(Child 2) is NOT listening.

(Child 1) IS working on _____.

(Child 2) is NOT working on _____.

TRANSITIONS

(Child 1) IS ready to go to (gym).

(Child 2) is NOT ready to go.

ICPS Words: Is-Not

Integrating ICPS concepts in the curriculum helps extend them to children's academic functioning. Try applying the concepts to the specific content areas you are currently teaching.

NEWS AND EVENTS OF THE DAY

Today IS (Tuesday). Today is NOT _____.

(On a rainy day) It IS sunny outside.

It is NOT?

Oh, I tried to trick you. It is NOT sunny. It is _____.

Who IS here today?

Who is NOT here today?

READING AND STORY COMPREHENSION

This IS the letter *(e)*.

(On chalkboard or child's worksheet) Show me a letter that is NOT a *(p)*.

(From any story) One person in the story I just read to you IS a (police officer).

(He/she) is NOT a _____.

The (police officer) in this story did three things. *(Show three fingers.)*

Which one did (he/she) NOT do?

For example:

* Help a child who fell.
* Take a man to the hospital.
* Help a woman cross the street.
* Blow a whistle very loud.

MATH

This IS a (square). It is NOT a (diamond).

What else is it NOT?

What numbers are on the chalkboard? (*Write:* 1–2–4–7–8.)

What numbers are NOT on the board? Which ones are missing?

2 + 2 IS 4.

2 + 2 is NOT _____.

If children are capable, repeat for 2 × 2 and 2 − 2, as well as for other number combinations.

SOCIAL STUDIES

_____ IS the name of our (city/town). It is NOT the name of our _____. (*If needed:* Country or state?)

What does a mother do in a family that a 5-year-old does NOT do?

What can you do at a football game that you can NOT do in church?

SCIENCE

This IS a leaf. This is NOT a _____.

This IS (September). It is NOT _____.

It IS (sunny/raining/snowing) outside today.

What happens in the winter that does NOT happen in the summer? (*If needed:* Does it snow or rain?)

MUSIC

Show me an instrument that IS a (drum).

Show me an instrument that is NOT a (xylophone).

Or-And

PURPOSE

To suggest through these word concepts that there is more than one way to think about things

MATERIALS

Pictures from magazines, picture cards, or available classroom objects (for example, chalk, toys, books)

TEACHER SCRIPT

Today's ICPS words are OR and AND.

Is my name _____ OR is it Ms. Smith?

(*To Child 1*) Is your name _____ OR is your name Peter?

(Child 2), are you wearing a dress OR are you wearing pants?

(Child 3), are you a (for example, kindergartner) OR a (second grader)?

Repeat with several children, then place pictures or classroom objects in the middle of the floor.

Who can find a (horse) AND a (rabbit)?

Who can find a (dog) OR a (kitten)?

Show me something that is NOT a (monkey).

(Child 4), come up and hold a piece of chalk.

Now put it down.

Now pick up the piece of chalk AND an eraser.

Now put down the eraser but NOT the pencil.

(Child 5), pick up a book AND a pencil.

Put the book down but NOT the pencil.

Now put down the pencil.

(To Child 6) Are you wearing shoes AND socks OR shoes but NOT socks?

(To Child 7) Point to a desk OR a chair but NOT to a desk AND a chair.

Make up your own examples or let a child be the leader and make some up.

HINT

If a child is teasing with silly answers, casually say, "Oh, I know you're just teasing me." For a summary of suggestions for working with this and other "difficult" behaviors, see Appendix D.

ICPS Words: Or-And

JUICETIME/LUNCHTIME

Are you drinking (milk) OR (apple juice)?

Are you NOT drinking (milk) OR NOT drinking (apple juice)?

Show me a (glass) AND a (plate).

Is this (spinach) green OR is it _____?

It IS (green). It is NOT _____.

LINING UP

Are you going to (recess) OR to (gym)?

Does _____ have on a (white shirt) AND (brown pants) OR a (white shirt) AND (red pants)?

FREE PLAY

(Child 1) IS standing AND (he/she) IS _____.

(He/she) is NOT _____.

Are (Child 1) AND (Child 2) (painting) OR are (Child 1) AND (Child 3) (painting)? Who is NOT (painting)?

LISTENING AND PARTICIPATING

Is (Child 1) listening OR NOT listening?

(Child 2) AND (Child 3) are listening.

Is (Child 1) OR (Child 2) listening?

Is (Child 1) working on _____ OR talking to (his/her) neighbor?

TRANSITIONS

Are you ready to go to (gym) OR NOT ready to go to (gym)?

(Child 1) AND (Child 2) are ready to go to (gym).

(Child 3) is NOT ready.

(Child 3), are you NOT ready because you are (fussing) OR because you are (sitting)?

ICPS Words: Or-And

NEWS AND EVENTS OF THE DAY

Is today (Tuesday) OR is today (Wednesday)?

Is today (October 21st) OR (October 29th)?

Is _____ President of the United States OR of Mexico?

Where else is President _____ NOT the president?

READING AND STORY COMPREHENSION

Show me a capital *(G)* AND a lowercase *(g)*.

Show me the *(b)*, the *(t)*, AND the *(r)*.

Show me the *(c)* OR the *(f)*, but NOT the *(t)*.

Is this a *(b)* OR a *(c)*?

Did the (boy) in the story I just read to you (run away) OR did he (come home)?

MATH

Is this a (square) OR is this a (circle)?

Are these a (square) AND a (diamond) OR a (square) AND a (circle)?

Show me a (triangle) AND a (rectangle).

Show me a 1 OR a 2.

Show me a 3 AND a 4, but NOT a 5.

SOCIAL STUDIES

The colors of the American flag are red, white, AND _____.

They are NOT red, white, AND _____.

Who puts fires out, a fire fighter OR a mail carrier?

What does a mail carrier do that a fire fighter does NOT do?

SCIENCE

A flower grows. But to grow, it needs _____ AND _____.
(*If needed:* Water AND sun OR water AND marbles?)

What else does it need? Water AND sun AND _____?

Are the leaves on the trees in winter OR in summer?

Will this (feather) float OR sink if I put it in water?

MUSIC

Show me a triangle AND a drum, but NOT a horn.

Do–Do Not

PURPOSE

To help children learn to listen and later be able to take in information to avoid faulty conclusions

MATERIALS

None

TEACHER SCRIPT

Today's ICPS game is a new game with the word NOT. It is called the Do–Do Not Game.

Listen carefully. If I say do something, then do what I say.

If I say do tap your knee, tap your knee. *(Demonstrate.)*

If I say do NOT do something, just sit still.

If I say do NOT tap your knee, just stay still.

OK. Are you ready?

Do NOT tap your knee. *(Pause.)*

Good, you just stayed still because I said do NOT.

Listen carefully. Sometimes I'm going to say do and sometimes I'm going to say do NOT.

Do pat your head. *(Pat your head.)*

Do stamp your foot. *(Stamp your foot.)*

Do NOT rub your tummy. *(Rub your tummy.)*

Alternate "do" and "do NOT" with additional actions—for example, rolling your arms, laughing, clapping your hands, crying, standing up, and so forth. Let a few children lead the activity as time permits. You may whisper ideas to them if needed.

HINT

If a child accidentally performs an opposite instruction, just laugh and say, "Oh, _____ missed."

If I Say

PURPOSE

Like Lesson 3, to help children learn to listen and later be able to take in information to avoid faulty conclusions

MATERIALS

None

TEACHER SCRIPT

Today we're going to play the Do–Do Not Game in a new way.

We're going to call today's game the If I Say Game.

Here is how we will play.

I'm going to say a word. The word is *head.* Can you show me your head? *(Let children respond.)*

Good. Now if I say the word *head,* you do point to your head.

I'm going to say lots of other words, too. Like *leg.* But only point to your head if I say *head.*

If I say *leg,* do NOT point to your leg—just sit still.

Point only if I say *head.* You'll get the idea when we play.

Leg: Good, you did NOT point to your leg. We only point to our heads when I say the word *head.*

Arm: Good, you did NOT point to your arm, because we are pointing only when we hear the word *head.*

Head: Good, you pointed to your head, because I said the word *head.*

Continue the game by saying these words: knee, eye, head, ear, *and* foot. *Then change the word to listen for.*

Do NOT point to your head anymore.

Now we will listen for a new word. The word is *knee.*

Play the game as long as time and interest permit, changing the word to listen for as desired.

Who Am I Thinking Of?

PURPOSE

To review the ICPS words NOT and AND, as well as to encourage listening and paying attention

MATERIALS

None

TEACHER SCRIPT

I am thinking of someone in this room.

I am NOT thinking of a boy.

Who am I NOT thinking of?

Good, I am NOT thinking of (Child 1) because (Child 1) IS a boy.

Who else am I NOT thinking of?

Yes, I am NOT thinking of (Child 2) because (Child 2) IS a boy.

Next select a child by identifying an article of clothing that only that child has on.

I am thinking of a girl.

I am thinking of a girl with a (red dress) on.

Who am I NOT thinking of?

Right, I am NOT thinking of _____ because _____ does NOT have a (red dress) on.

Who else am I NOT thinking of?

Who am I thinking of?

Next pick something that at least two children are wearing.

I am thinking of a boy.

I am NOT thinking of a girl.

I am thinking of a boy with a (blue shirt) on.

What boy am I NOT thinking of?

Right, I am NOT thinking of _____ because _____ does NOT have a (blue shirt) on.

33

Tell me, who does have a (blue shirt) on?

Yes, _____ AND _____ have (blue shirts) on.

If a child names someone whose shirt has, for example, a blue stripe, reinforce by saying, "His shirt does have some blue on it. I'm glad you were thinking. Now look to see whose shirt is all blue."

If I am thinking of a boy with a (blue shirt) on, then I am thinking of either _____ OR _____.

I am thinking of only one of them.

I am thinking of a boy who has a (blue shirt) AND (brown pants) on. Who am I thinking of?

Yes, I am thinking of _____ because _____ has on a (blue shirt) AND (brown pants).

What boy has on a (blue shirt) but NOT (brown pants)?

HINT

If a shy nonresponder verbally parrots another child, do not insist on a different answer at this time. Simply say, "Good, you told us, too." The child is thus reinforced for saying something.

Some-All

PURPOSE

To encourage later appreciation that a particular solution will satisfy SOME but not ALL people—or SOME but not ALL of the time

MATERIALS

Chalkboard or easel

TEACHER SCRIPT

Draw five circles, as shown.

I'm drawing circles on the chalkboard.　　○ ○ ○ ○ ○

I'm filling in SOME of them in row 2.　　● ● ● ○ ○

I did not fill in ALL of them.

Now I'm going to fill in ALL of them in Row 3.　● ● ● ● ●

Now I'm going to do this. *(Erase some.)*　● ● ○ ○ ○

Did I fill in SOME or ALL of them?

Look at row 4. Now this. *(Fill in more.)*　● ● ● ● ○

SOME or ALL?

Everybody stand up.
Are ALL the children in this class standing up OR are SOME of them standing up?
OK, now everybody sit down.

Now (Child 1), (Child 2), and (Child 3), stand up AND touch your heads.

(Child 4), (Child 5), and (Child 6), stand up but do NOT touch your heads.

(To the group) Are ALL the children who are standing up touching their heads OR are SOME of them touching their heads?

Now (Child 4), (Child 5), and (Child 6), touch your heads.

(Child 1), (Child 2), and (Child 3), keep your hands on your heads.

(To the group) Now are ALL the children who are standing up touching their heads, OR are SOME of them touching their heads?

Who can name ALL the children in this room who have (red tops) on?

Now tell me SOME but NOT ALL the children who have (blue tops) on.

(Child 7), (Child 8), and (Child 9), come up here and fold your arms.

(Child 10), (Child 11), and (Child 12), come up here, fold your arms, AND cross your feet, like this. *(Demonstrate.)*

(To the group) Which children are folding their arms AND crossing their feet?

Which children are folding their arms but NOT crossing their feet?

HINT

Let shy nonresponders who are not comfortable talking participate in movement (for example, touching their heads or folding their arms). Movement is a first step toward decreasing inhibition.

More Some-All

PURPOSE

To strengthen later appreciation that a particular solution will satisfy SOME but not ALL people—or SOME but not ALL of the time

MATERIALS

Illustration 1

Classroom objects (for example, toys, books, crayons)

TEACHER SCRIPT

Show children Illustration 1. You may copy or enlarge the illustration and display it so children can see and point to it easily during the lesson. Alternatively, you may place the illustration under an opaque projector or give each child a copy to keep and color, if desired.

(Child 1), show me SOME of the boys. Be careful. Show me SOME, NOT ALL, of the boys.

(Child 2), show me SOME of the girls.

(Child 3), show me ALL of the children who are holding something in their hands.

(Child 4), show me ALL of the children who are sitting down and NOT holding something.

(Child 5), show me a girl who is NOT wearing a skirt.

(To the group) Are ALL the children standing OR are SOME children standing?

Are ALL the girls wearing skirts OR are SOME girls wearing skirts?

Have children come up to the front. Give some of them objects. Repeat the line of questioning suggested for the illustration.

ILLUSTRATION 1 Lesson 7

ICPS Words: Some-All

JUICETIME/LUNCHTIME

Tell me SOME of the boys at this table.

Tell me ALL of the boys at this table.

Who are SOME of the girls at this table?

Who are ALL of the girls at this table?

Tell me SOME of the children who have on (red) tops.

Tell me ALL of the children who have on (blue) tops.

Tell me SOME children who do NOT have on (blue) tops.

LINING UP

Are SOME of you in this class standing in line OR are ALL of you in this class standing in line?

FREE PLAY

Tell me SOME children who are (painting).

Tell me ALL the children who are (painting).

Show me SOME of the (red crayons) on this table.

Show me ALL of the (blue crayons) on this table.

Show me ALL of the crayons that are NOT (red).

LISTENING AND PARTICIPATING

Are SOME of you listening OR are ALL of you listening?

Are SOME of you (working on your numbers) OR are ALL of you?

TRANSITIONS

Are SOME of you ready to go to (gym) OR are ALL of you ready?

Are SOME of you (standing quietly in line) OR are ALL of you?

ICPS Words: Some-All

NEWS AND EVENTS OF THE DAY

Who thinks today IS (Tuesday)?

Did ALL of you raise your hands OR did SOME of you?

It IS (raining) in our (city/town) today.

Is it (raining) in ALL (cities/towns) today?

READING AND STORY COMPREHENSION

Show me ALL the capital letters on this page.

Show me SOME of the lowercase letters.

Do ALL of these words have a short *a* sound OR do SOME of these words have a short *a* sound? (*For example:* Cat, fan, gate, tap, tape, car.)

Which words do NOT have a short *a* sound?

In the story I just read to you, did ALL of the (kids in the house fight) OR did SOME of them?

MATH

Show me ALL the (squares) on this page. Show me SOME (diamonds).

Show me SOME shapes on this page that are NOT (circles).

Show me ALL the shapes that are NOT (circles).

Show me ALL the (1s) on this page AND ALL the (2s).

Show me SOME of the numbers that are NOT (1s).

Show me ALL the number combinations that add up to 6.

1 + 5   2 + 3   6 + 0   1 + 2   3 + 1 + 2

SOCIAL STUDIES

Do ALL of us OR SOME of us walk to school?

Raise your hand if your mother works outside your home.

Raise your hand if your mother does NOT work outside your home.

Do SOME mothers OR ALL mothers work outside your homes?

SCIENCE

Show me ALL the leaves on this plant.

Show me SOME of the leaves on this plant.

Will ALL of these objects float OR will SOME float?

Which ones will NOT float?

MUSIC

Show me ALL the instruments that have strings.

Show me SOME of the instruments that have strings.

Show me an instrument that is NOT shaped like a triangle.

If-Then

PURPOSE

To help children in later consequential thinking: "IF I do this, THEN that might happen"

MATERIALS

None

TEACHER SCRIPT

IF I am thinking of a girl, THEN I am NOT thinking of a _____.

IF I am NOT thinking of a boy, THEN I am thinking of a _____.

IF I point to (Child 1), THEN I am NOT pointing to _____.

Who else am I NOT pointing to?

Everybody stand up.

Everybody stretch, hands up, like this. *(Demonstrate.)*

IF we keep stretching, THEN we are NOT sleeping.

What else are we NOT doing?

Now everybody stand on one foot.

IF you are standing on one foot, THEN you are NOT standing on _____.

Make up other exercises or stretches as time and interest permit.

ICPS Words: If-Then

JUICETIME/LUNCHTIME

IF we are drinking (juice), THEN we are NOT drinking _____.

IF this IS a (hamburger), THEN it is NOT a _____.

IF we are sitting at this table, THEN we are NOT sitting on the _____.
(*If needed:* Floor OR ceiling?)

LINING UP

IF this IS the boys' line, THEN it is NOT the _____.

IF this is NOT the boys' line, THEN it IS the _____.

IF we are lining up to go to (recess), THEN we are NOT lining up to
go to _____.

FREE PLAY

IF (Child 1) IS (painting), THEN (he/she) is NOT _____.

IF (Child 2) is NOT (building with blocks), THEN (he/she) IS _____.

IF it IS (raining), THEN can we OR can we NOT go outside for recess?

LISTENING AND PARTICIPATING

IF _____ is NOT listening, THEN (he/she) can NOT learn what we
are working on now.

We are working on _____.

We are working on our (numbers) now.

IF _____ IS talking to (his/her) neighbor, THEN (he/she) is NOT
working on _____.

TRANSITIONS

We are getting ready to go to (gym).

_____ IS (making noise).

IF _____ IS (making noise), THEN (he/she) is NOT ready
to go to (gym).

ICPS Words: If-Then

NEWS AND EVENTS OF THE DAY

IF today IS (Tuesday), THEN it is NOT _____.

IF it IS (September), THEN it is NOT _____.

IF it IS (raining) outside today, THEN will we have recess inside OR outside?

READING AND STORY COMPREHENSION

IF this IS the letter *(g)*, THEN it is NOT the letter _____ OR the letter _____.

IF the child in the story I just read (went to the circus), THEN (he/she) did NOT go to the _____.

MATH

IF 2 + 2 IS 4, THEN 2 + 2 is NOT _____.

Use if-then to narrow down concepts. For example:

IF this is NOT a circle, THEN IS it a diamond OR a square?

IF this is NOT a circle OR a square, THEN it IS a _____.

SOCIAL STUDIES

IF you do NOT walk to school, THEN you _____.

IF you live in the city, THEN you do NOT live in the _____.

SCIENCE

IF this rock is very, very heavy and I put in into water, THEN it will _____. (*If needed:* Float OR sink?)

IF this plant does NOT get any water, THEN what will happen to it?

Same-Different

PURPOSE

To help children later recognize that there are DIFFERENT ways to solve the SAME problem

MATERIALS

None

TEACHER SCRIPT

Today's ICPS words are SAME and DIFFERENT. Watch me.

I'm raising my hand. *(Raise hand, lower, then raise again.)*

I raised my hand again. I just did the SAME thing. I raised my hand.

Now I'm going to do something DIFFERENT.

I'm going to tap my knee. *(Demonstrate.)*

See, tapping my knee *(keep tapping)* is DIFFERENT from raising my hand *(raise hand).*

I'm tapping my knee. *(Tap knee.)*

Can you ALL do the SAME thing?

_____, can you do something that is NOT the SAME as tapping your knee? *(Let the child respond.)*

Good. That is NOT the SAME as tapping your knee.

OK, let's have more fun with the words SAME and DIFFERENT.

Let's ALL do the SAME thing.

First, stamp your feet.

Alternate asking some-all children to do the same-different thing: roll arms, tap head, stretch, and so forth.

HINT

If a child is behaving obstinately or disruptively, do not exclude her. Instead, use ICPS words to bring her into the game. Say, for example:

- Is _____ playing our game OR is _____ NOT playing our game?

- Is _____ doing the SAME thing OR something DIFFERENT?

- *(If the child is sitting and making noise)* We are jumping.
  Is _____ doing the SAME thing OR something DIFFERENT?

Encourage the shy nonresponder to come up to the front and illustrate, with body motions, something that is the same as or different from what you are telling the group to do. Many such children enjoy participating in this way.

More Same-Different

PURPOSE

To strengthen later awareness that there are DIFFERENT ways to solve the SAME problem

MATERIALS

None

TEACHER SCRIPT

(To the group) Are (Child 1) AND (Child 2) wearing the SAME color top OR a DIFFERENT color top?

Who has on the SAME color top as (Child 1)?

OK, now we're going to play a guessing game.

I'm going to tell children to stand up who ALL have something about them that is the SAME.

Name the girls in the class, asking each one to stand up.

What is the SAME about ALL the children standing up?

How are the children sitting down DIFFERENT from those who are standing up?

Let children guess the answer. Next name children wearing a particular color, asking each one to stand.

What is the SAME about ALL the children standing up that is DIFFERENT from those who are sitting down? *(If needed:* It is NOT whether someone is a boy or a girl. It IS something that ALL who are standing are wearing.*)*

Let children guess the answer. Next name the children who are not wearing sneakers, asking each one to stand.

What do ALL the children standing up NOT have on that those sitting down do have on?

Let children guess the answer. Next use two criteria, such as red shirts and white socks.

Now I'm going to make this even harder. What two things do ALL the children standing up have on that those sitting down do NOT have on?

Think of three things, if the class can be so challenged. You may wish to let a child be the leader. If so, have the child whisper what he or she is doing so you can help.

Next I'm going to point to two things that are the SAME.

You tell me how they are the SAME.

Point to two things that are, for example, red or square.

Who can point to two things that are the SAME but NOT the ones that I just pointed to? Then I'll guess how they are the SAME.

Now I'll point to three things that are the SAME, and you tell me how they are the SAME.

Expand as far as the class can handle, having different children point to three things that are the same, and so on. Have the children whisper to you how the objects are the same, then let the rest of the group guess.

Is there someone in this room who has the SAME first name as you?

Does anyone have the SAME last name as you?

Is there someone whose first name begins with the SAME first letter as yours? *(Give an example, if necessary.)*

How about your last name? SAME first letter?

Two Things at the Same Time

PURPOSE

To encourage appreciation that adults cannot always do two things at the SAME time

MATERIALS

None

TEACHER SCRIPT

Now we're going to play the Two Things at the Same Time Game.

A couple of days ago, some of you stood up in front AND folded your arms AND crossed your feet at the SAME time, like this. *(Demonstrate.)*

I can do other things at the SAME time.

I can raise my hand AND stamp my foot at the SAME time, like this. *(Demonstrate.)*

(Child 1), come up here and show me two things you can do at the SAME time. *(If needed:* For instance, you can laugh AND rub your tummy at the SAME time.)

(To Child 2) What two things can you do at the SAME time? _____ AND _____.

If a child imitates another: Can you think of two DIFFERENT things you can do at the SAME time? *(If needed:* Tap your head AND _____.)

(To the group) There are some things I can NOT do at the SAME time.

I can NOT talk, like this—hello!—AND sing, like this—fa, la la!—at the SAME time.

What two things can you NOT do at the SAME time?

If needed: Laugh AND _____.

If still needed: Can you laugh *(laugh)* AND scream at the SAME time? No, you can NOT laugh AND scream at the SAME time.

Let children give several examples.

Can I teach you arithmetic AND spelling at the SAME time?

Can I teach ALL of you arithmetic AND talk to one of you who is bothering someone else at the SAME time?

IF I call on one of you and ALL of you shout out at the SAME time, THEN can I hear the person I called on?

Bring up any other problem areas you'd like to discuss with your class.

What can you do at the SAME time in class? (*For example:* Sit in your seat AND listen to me.)

What can you NOT do in class at the SAME time? (*For example:* Talk to your friend AND work on your lesson.)

What about two things I can NOT do at the SAME time? (*For example:* Listen to you AND to four other children.)

HINT

Offer the shy nonresponder a choice—for example, "Can you sit down AND jump at the SAME time?" Encourage the child to shake her head no with you.

ICPS Words: Same-Different

JUICETIME/LUNCHTIME

This IS (milk). This IS a (cookie).

Are (milk) AND (cookies) the SAME thing OR something DIFFERENT?

Who likes (chicken)?

Who does NOT like (chicken)?

Do (Child 1) AND (Child 2) like the SAME thing OR something DIFFERENT?

Can you eat a (hamburger) AND drink (juice) at the SAME time?

LINING UP

ALL children who have on the SAME color as (for example, Child 1's shirt), get in line.

Those of you whose shoes are DIFFERENT from (sneakers), get in line.

FREE PLAY

(Child 1) IS (coloring). (Child 2) IS (working with clay).

Are (Child 1) AND (Child 2) doing the SAME thing OR something DIFFERENT?

(Child 2) AND (Child 3) are doing the SAME thing.

Who is doing something DIFFERENT?

Tell me two (or three or four) children who are doing the SAME thing.

Can you (play checkers) AND (jump rope) at the SAME time?

LISTENING AND PARTICIPATING

Are ALL of you listening OR are SOME of you doing something DIFFERENT?

IF ALL of you talk at the SAME time, THEN can I hear what _____ is saying?

Are ALL of you (writing your letters) OR are SOME of you doing something DIFFERENT?

Can you (write your letters) AND talk to your neighbor at the SAME time?

Is _____ doing the SAME thing as the rest of us OR something DIFFERENT?

TRANSITIONS

(If a child is talking, disrupting the line) Is the boys' line the SAME as the girls' line?

How are they DIFFERENT?

What can you do so the two lines will be the SAME?

MINI-DIALOGUE

The following example shows how you can incorporate ICPS word concepts when problems between children come up.

Situation: Annie grabs a toy airplane from Russ.

Teacher: *(To Russ)* What happened? What's the matter?

Russ: She took my plane!

Teacher: *(To Annie)* What do you think happened?

Annie: He's already had a long turn!

Teacher: *(To both)* Do you see what happened the SAME way OR a DIFFERENT way?

Russ: DIFFERENT.

Teacher: It looks as though we have a problem. How can you solve it? Make it better?

Annie: Let's play together.

Teacher: *(To Russ)* Is that OK with you?

If yes: Go ahead and try that.

If no: Which of you can think of something DIFFERENT?

ICPS Words: Same-Different

NEWS AND EVENTS OF THE DAY

Ask children to tell the group something about themselves. Write their answers on chalkboard or easel. For example:

Andre IS going to move.

John IS going to the park with his dad.

Rose IS going to take pictures.

(Child 1), find the SAME word as this *(point to the word IS and ask the child to circle it.)*

(After child circles one instance) Where else is the SAME word?

(Child 2), find a DIFFERENT word and circle it.

(To the group) Who sees the SAME word that (Child 2) circled?
(Or: IS there OR is there NOT another place where you see the SAME word?)

READING AND STORY COMPREHENSION

Is the sound of the letter *a* in *cat* the SAME OR DIFFERENT from the sound of the letter *a* in *gate*?

Color ALL the pictures that start with the SAME sound as *(n)*.

Color two pictures that start with a DIFFERENT sound.

Do these two words mean the SAME thing OR something DIFFERENT? *(For example:* Big/huge, tall/short, poquito/little, bonita/pretty.)

If a child says the words mean something different, ask why. If, for example, a child says huge is bigger than big, give praise for good thinking.

MATH

Activity 1

Draw the following sequence of shapes on chalkboard or easel.

Show me a shape that is NOT the SAME as a circle.

Color ALL the circles the SAME color.

Color ALL the squares the SAME color but a color that is DIFFERENT from the circles.

Find two triangles. Color each of them a DIFFERENT color.

Activity 2

Write the sequence 1–1–1–2–2–2–3–3–3 on chalkboard or easel, or lay plastic or wooden numerals on a table.

Show me two numbers that are the SAME AND one number that is DIFFERENT.

Activity 3

Are the answers to these number combinations the SAME OR are they DIFFERENT?

2 + 5   4 + 3   1 + 6   3 + 4   6 + 1

Which number combination equals something DIFFERENT?

0 + 4   2 + 2   3 + 1   4 + 1   1 + 3

How are ☐ and ☐ DIFFERENT?

How are they the SAME?

SOCIAL STUDIES

What do fire fighters do?

They put out fires AND _____.

What do police officers do?

_____ AND _____.

Can you think of something that fire fighters AND police officers do that is the SAME?

What do they do that is DIFFERENT?

What do a nurse AND a doctor do that are the SAME?

SCIENCE

How is rain DIFFERENT from snow?

How are they the SAME?

How are winter and summer DIFFERENT?

How are a train AND a car the SAME? (*For example:* They both have wheels, both move.)

How are they DIFFERENT?

How are a horse AND a zebra the SAME?

How are they DIFFERENT?

The mama cat just had a baby dog.

No? I tried to trick you. Why NOT?

MUSIC

How are a violin and a guitar the SAME?

How are they DIFFERENT?

Before-After

PURPOSE

To help with later consequential thinking—for example, "He hit me AFTER I hit him"

MATERIALS

None

TEACHER SCRIPT

Our ICPS words today are BEFORE and AFTER.

First, we're going to talk about the word BEFORE.

I'm tapping my knee. *(Demonstrate.)*

Now I'm patting my head. *(Demonstrate.)*

I tapped my knee first.

I tapped my knee BEFORE I patted my head.

Did I tap my knee BEFORE I patted my head?

Yes, BEFORE.

I'm rolling my arms. *(Demonstrate.)*

I'm stamping my feet. *(Demonstrate.)*

Did I roll my arms BEFORE I stamped my feet?

Yes, BEFORE.

(To Child 1) Now you do something. *(Let the child respond.)*

Now do something DIFFERENT.

What did you do first?

Did you do that BEFORE you _____?

Yes, BEFORE.

Now think of something else to do.

And one more thing.

What did you do first?

Did you _____ BEFORE you _____?

Yes, BEFORE.

(To the group) When you put your shoes and socks on, which do you put on first? *(Let children respond.)*

Yes, your socks.

Do you put your socks on BEFORE your shoes?

Yes, BEFORE.

(To the group) Tell me what you do BEFORE you come to school in the morning. *(Let children respond.)*

That's one thing.

What else do you do?

That's two things.

Can you think of a third thing?

Now we're going to talk about the word AFTER.

I'm tapping my knee. *(Demonstrate.)*

Now I'm patting my head. *(Demonstrate.)*

I tapped my knee first—BEFORE I patted my head.

Now listen carefully.

I patted my head second—AFTER I tapped my knee.

Did I pat my head AFTER I tapped my knee?

Yes, AFTER.

(To Child 2) Now you do something. *(Let the child respond.)*

Now do something DIFFERENT.

What did you do first?

What did you do second?

Did you _____ AFTER you _____?

Yes, AFTER.

Repeat with as many children as time and interest permit.

Before-After, Now-Later

PURPOSE

To help children with later consequential thinking and with later appreciation of the importance of timing when making decisions

MATERIALS

Chalkboard or easel

TEACHER SCRIPT

Today's ICPS game starts with more about the words BEFORE and AFTER. Watch me carefully.

I'm writing on the chalkboard. I did that first.

Next, I'm erasing what I wrote.

I wrote on the board BEFORE I erased what I wrote.

I wrote on the board first.

Did I write on the board BEFORE I erased what I wrote?

Yes, BEFORE.

I wrote on the board. Then what happened next?

Did I erase the board AFTER I wrote on it?

AFTER is what happens next.

I wrote on the board. Then I erased what I wrote.

Did I write on the board BEFORE or AFTER I erased what I wrote?

Did I erase the board BEFORE or AFTER I wrote on it?

Now watch me. There is something I have to do BEFORE I can even write on the board.

Very dramatically, pick up the chalk.

What did I just do?

Yes, I picked up the chalk.

Next, I'm writing on the board.

Did I pick up the chalk BEFORE or AFTER I wrote on the board?

(To Child 1) You come up now and be leader. *(Whisper to the child:* Draw a circle on the board. Now draw a square.*)*

(To the group) Did (Child 1) draw a circle BEFORE or AFTER (he/she) drew a square?

Have children tell the leader what to put on the board (for example, numbers, letters, shapes).

(To Child 2) Open the door.

Now come and stand in front of the class.

Now go and close the door.

Did (Child 2) open the door BEFORE or AFTER (he/she) stood in front of the class?

Expand the number of directions to four, five, and so on.

Here are some new words to think about:

We are playing our ICPS game NOW.

What are we doing NOW?

Yes, we are playing our ICPS game.

LATER, it will be time for (lunch/recess).

Is it time for (lunch/recess) NOW or LATER?

Are we playing our ICPS game BEFORE or AFTER we go to (lunch/recess)?

Yes, BEFORE. We will go to lunch LATER, AFTER we finish our game.

It is daytime NOW.

It will be night LATER.

IF it is daytime NOW, THEN it is light outside.

LATER, when it will be night, it will be _____.
(If needed: Light OR dark?*)*

ICPS Words: Before-After, Now-Later

JUICETIME/LUNCHTIME

Do you eat your dessert BEFORE or AFTER you eat your _____?

We are having (juice/lunch) NOW. What will we do LATER?

Do we (have juice/eat lunch) BEFORE or AFTER we go home?

Do we clean up our table BEFORE or AFTER we (have juice/eat lunch)?

LINING UP

You are going to (gym) NOW.

Do you go to (gym) BEFORE or AFTER our (spelling lesson)?

ALL children with (blue tops) on line up.

ALL children with (red tops) on line up.

Did those with (red tops) on line up BEFORE or AFTER those with (blue tops) on?

FREE PLAY

SOME of you can (paint) NOW.

SOME of you will have to wait until LATER.

If you (paint) NOW, will you (paint) BEFORE or AFTER the next group?

LISTENING AND PARTICIPATING

Do you know what to do BEFORE you listen to me tell you or AFTER?

IF you (do/do NOT) get your work done NOW, THEN you (will/will NOT) be ready for recess LATER.

TRANSITIONS

You are going to (recess) NOW.

What do you do BEFORE you leave your desk?
(*For example:* You put your books away.)

Do you put on your jacket BEFORE or AFTER you go outside?

Do you hang your jacket up BEFORE or AFTER you sit down at your desk?

MINI-DIALOGUE

Situation: Brad is engaged in nagging, demanding behavior.

Brad: *(To the teacher)* I want to fingerpaint.

Teacher: I can't get the fingerpaints NOW. We're going outside soon.

Brad: I don't want to go outside. I want to fingerpaint.

Teacher: You can't stay inside because no one can stay here with you. Can you think of something DIFFERENT to do NOW?

Brad: *(Angrily)* No!

Teacher: I know you want to fingerpaint. I bet if you think very hard, you can think of something DIFFERENT to do NOW. Maybe you can fingerpaint LATER.

Brad: *(Thinks a minute.)* OK, I'll play with Michael.

In this exchange, the teacher helps the child cope with the frustration of not being able to have what he wanted right away. Had the teacher suggested he draw with crayons, or do something else, the child would likely have resisted more.

ICPS Words: Before-After, Now-Later

NEWS AND EVENTS OF THE DAY

_____, tell us two things you did today.

Did you _____ BEFORE or AFTER you _____?

What are you doing NOW? (*If needed:* Standing OR sitting, talking OR singing, and so forth.)

Today is (Thursday).

Yesterday was _____.

Does (Thursday) come BEFORE or AFTER (Wednesday)?

Does (Friday) come BEFORE or AFTER (Thursday)?

READING AND STORY COMPREHENSION

Does the letter *c* come BEFORE or AFTER the letter *d*?

Tell me SOME letters that come BEFORE *d*.

Tell me ALL the letters that come BEFORE *d*.

What letters come AFTER *x*? _____ AND _____?

What letter comes BEFORE *c* AND AFTER *a*?

In the dictionary, which of these words comes BEFORE the word *cat:* apple, pen, top, car, city?

Which of these words comes AFTER the word *cat?*

In the story I just read, did (the girl help the neighbor) BEFORE or AFTER (she helped her mother)?

MATH

Activity 1

Does the number 1 come BEFORE or AFTER the number 2?

What comes AFTER the number 4?

Tell me a number that does NOT come BEFORE 5.

Tell me a number that does come BEFORE 5.

Tell me SOME numbers that come BEFORE 5.

Tell me ALL the numbers that come BEFORE 5.

IF the number 1 comes BEFORE the number 2, THEN it does NOT come _____? (*If needed:* BEFORE or AFTER?)

Activity 2

Was your mother born BEFORE or AFTER your grandmother? (*If needed:* Who was born first?)

If a 5-year-old (or 6- or 7-year-old) boy has a 10-year-old sister, was the sister born BEFORE or AFTER the boy?

Expand to more than two siblings; ask children about their own siblings.

Activity 3

It is (morning) NOW. It will be (night) LATER.

Does (morning) come BEFORE or AFTER (night)?

It is (9:30) NOW. It will be (10:30) LATER.

Does (9:30) come BEFORE or AFTER (10:30)?

If the child says AFTER in either of these cases, meaning the next day, say, "That's true. Good thinking." Ask, for example, "On the SAME day, does morning come BEFORE or AFTER night?"

Does first grade come BEFORE or AFTER second grade?

IF first grade comes BEFORE second grade, THEN it does NOT come _____. (*If needed:* BEFORE or AFTER?)

SOCIAL STUDIES

Are you a 5-year-old (or 6- or 7-year-old) BEFORE or AFTER you are a baby?

IF a 5-year-old (or 6- or 7-year-old) has an older brother, does the brother go to bed BEFORE or AFTER the 5-year-old (or 6- or 7-year-old)?

Abraham Lincoln was the sixteenth President of the United States.

George Washington was the first President of the United States.

Was Abraham Lincoln President BEFORE or AFTER George Washington?

Abraham Lincoln wanted ALL Americans to be free.

He lived from 1809 to 1865.

Martin Luther King was a civil rights leader.

He wanted ALL Americans to be free.

He lived from 1929 to 1968.

How were Abraham Lincoln AND Martin Luther King the SAME?

How were they DIFFERENT?

Did Abraham Lincoln live BEFORE or AFTER Martin Luther King?

SCIENCE

Does a plant grow BEFORE or AFTER you plant the seed?

Does water become ice BEFORE or AFTER you put it in the freezer?

What happens to water AFTER you take it out of the freezer?

Review of ICPS Words

PURPOSE

To strengthen understanding of ICPS words

MATERIALS

Chalkboard or easel

Paper and pencils

TEACHER SCRIPT

Point to a number of items of the same color, size, or shape.

How are the two (or three or four) things I am pointing to the SAME?

Who can show me (point to, touch):

Two (or three or four) things in this room that are the SAME color?

Two (or three or four) things in this room that are round?

Who can tell me:

ALL the girls who have (red tops) on?

SOME boys who have (blue tops) on?

ALL the boys who have (blue tops) on?

Who is wearing a (blue top) AND (brown pants)?

Who is wearing a (blue top) but NOT (brown pants)?

ALL the children whose first names are the SAME?

ALL the children whose last names are the SAME?

Who can point to:

The chalkboard BEFORE the desk?

The window AFTER the door?

Your desk BEFORE the floor?

Draw two identical shapes on the board.

I'm drawing on the board two things that are the SAME.

Take out paper and pencil.

Draw two things that are the SAME. You can draw anything you want.

Now draw two things that are DIFFERENT.

Draw a ball AND a stick.

Draw a ball OR a stick but NOT a ball AND a stick.

Draw something that is NOT a circle.

Review of ICPS Words: Is-Not, Or-And, Some-All, If-Then, Same-Different, Before-After, Now-Later

When a child interrupts:

Can I talk to _____ AND to you at the SAME time?

I am talking to _____ NOW. I can talk to you LATER.

I can talk to you AFTER I finish talking to _____.

Can you think of something DIFFERENT to do NOW?

When two children are arguing over a toy:

IF someone else is playing with that toy NOW, THEN can you play with it BEFORE or AFTER (he/she) has a turn?

IF you can NOT play with that toy NOW, THEN when can you play with it?

When a child disrupts the class:

Are ALL of you OR are SOME of you (doing the math lesson)?

Who IS doing the math lesson?

IS _____ doing the SAME thing OR something DIFFERENT from the rest of you?

YOUR IDEAS

Write down your own thoughts for applying these ICPS words in classroom interactions.

IS-NOT

_____

_____

_____

_____

_____

OR-AND

_____

_____

_____

_____

_____

SOME-ALL

_____

_____

_____

_____

_____

IF-THEN

_____

_____

_____

_____

_____

SAME-DIFFERENT

_____

_____

_____

_____

_____

BEFORE-AFTER

_____

_____

_____

_____

_____

NOW-LATER

_____

_____

_____

_____

_____

Review of ICPS Words: Is-Not, Or-And, Some-All, If-Then, Same-Different, Before-After, Now-Later

SCIENCE

This IS water. This IS ice.

This IS water AND _____.

IF I freeze this water, THEN it will NOT be the SAME. It will be _____. (*If needed:* The SAME or DIFFERENT?)

What will happen AFTER I freeze the water?

The water will turn to _____.

IF this is water NOW and I freeze it, THEN LATER it will be _____.

Will ALL of the water turn to ice OR will SOME of the water turn to ice?

What will happen AFTER I take the water out of the freezer if I leave this ice in the room for a long time?

Will ALL of the ice melt OR will SOME of it melt?

This is ice NOW. IF I melt it, THEN LATER it will be _____. It will NOT be _____.

NOW it IS (fall). It is NOT _____.

It is NOT _____ OR _____.

Who likes winter?

Who does NOT like winter?

Do ALL of you like winter OR do SOME of you like winter?

How is winter DIFFERENT from summer?

In the winter, do you put your boots on BEFORE or AFTER you go out in the snow?

CLASSIFICATION

The following activities use the ICPS word concepts SAME-DIFFERENT and NOT to encourage the idea that there is more than one way to classify things. Write the examples on chalkboard or easel and elicit the responses indicated.

Modes of Transportation

I'm going to write some things on the board. Tell me how they are the SAME.

Car

Truck

Bus

Boat

ANSWERS: All are forms of transportation; all are things to ride in; all move.

What else can you ride in? (*Possible responses:* An airplane, a wagon, a rocket.)

What is true of this next group of things?

Car

Truck

Bus

NOT a boat

What is DIFFERENT about a boat?

Tell me how a car, a truck, and a bus are the SAME.

ANSWERS: All move on the ground; all have wheels.

What about this next group of things? How are they the SAME?

> Bicycle
> Motorcycle
> Scooter

ANSWER: All have two wheels.

If needed, add the following to the previous list:

- NOT a bus
- NOT a car

Animals

I'm going to write some more things on the board. How are they the SAME?

> Bird
> Butterfly

ANSWER: Both can fly.

If needed, add the following to the previous list:

- NOT a zebra
- NOT a horse
- NOT a camel

If still needed, ask, "What can a bird AND a butterfly do that a zebra, a horse, AND a camel can NOT do?"

Now I'm going to change the question. How are these things the SAME?

Zebra

Horse

Camel

Whale

ANSWERS: All are living, nonhuman, warm-blooded, mammals.

(*After one response*) Good, how else are they the SAME? They are (for example, living) AND _____.

How else are they the SAME?

How is a camel DIFFERENT from a zebra AND a horse? (*Possible responses:* A camel lives in the desert, has humps, can live longer without water.)

Now watch. I'm going to change something.

Zebra

Horse

Camel

(*Point to all three items.*) How are these three the SAME?

ANSWER: All have four legs.

If needed, add the following to the list:

- NOT a man
- NOT a whale

If still needed, ask, "What do a zebra, a horse, AND a camel have that a whale and a man do NOT have?" For a further clue, add:

- Dog
- NOT a bird

(*After children have guessed the answer*) What else has four legs?

And what else?

A man, a whale, AND a bird do NOT have four legs. What other living creatures do NOT have four legs?

Use other criteria for classifying. For example:

- Reptiles, amphibians, mammals
- Pets, wild animals
- Egg-laying, non-egg-laying
- Warm-blooded, cold-blooded
- Living on land, desert, water

Foods

How are these things the SAME?

Apple
Raspberry
Strawberry
Orange

ANSWER: All are fruits.

If needed, add the following to the list:

- NOT steak

Steak is NOT a fruit.

What other food is NOT a fruit?

Now look carefully. What IS true of these? (*Point to the first three items. If needed:* How is an orange DIFFERENT from an apple, a raspberry, and a strawberry?)

Apple
Raspberry
Strawberry
NOT orange

ANSWER: All are red fruits.

Tell me something else that IS a fruit but is NOT red.

What about this? (*Point to the first two items. If needed:* What is true about an apple and an orange that is NOT true of a strawberry and a banana?)

Apple

Orange

NOT strawberry

NOT banana

ANSWER: Both are round.

Tell me another fruit that is NOT round.

Tell me something that is NOT a fruit that IS round.

YOUR IDEAS

Write down your own thoughts for applying these ICPS words in the curriculum.

IS-NOT

_____

_____

_____

_____

_____

OR-AND

_____

_____

_____

_____

_____

SOME-ALL

_____

_____

_____

_____

_____

IF-THEN

_____

_____

_____

_____

_____

SAME-DIFFERENT

_____

_____

_____

_____

_____

BEFORE-AFTER

_____

_____

_____

_____

_____

NOW-LATER

_____

_____

_____

_____

_____

How People Feel

PURPOSE

To help children identify people's HAPPY and SAD feelings, for later understanding of positive and negative consequences

MATERIALS

Any two hand puppets (for example, Dilly the Duck and Poppy the Pup)

TEACHER SCRIPT

Dilly: *(Open the puppet's mouth wide and laugh.)* I am laughing.

Poppy: *(Pull puppet's mouth in, put head down, and cry.)* I am crying.

Teacher: IF Dilly IS laughing *(make Dilly laugh)*, THEN he is NOT _____. *(If needed:* SAD.)

Dilly: IF I am laughing, I feel _____. *(Let children respond.)* Yes, IF I am laughing, I feel HAPPY.

Poppy: I am crying. I feel _____. *(Let children respond.)* Yes, IF I am crying, I feel SAD.

Teacher: Do Dilly AND Poppy feel the SAME way OR a DIFFERENT way? Yes, they feel a DIFFERENT way. They do NOT feel the SAME way.

How Can You Tell?

PURPOSE

To show children that there is more than one way to find out how someone feels or what someone likes—and that watching and listening are two of them

MATERIALS

A penny

TEACHER SCRIPT

Here are my eyes. *(Point to your eyes.)*

What can I do with my eyes?

Yes, I can see with my eyes.

These are my ears. *(Point to your ears.)*

What can I do with my ears that I can NOT do with my eyes?

Yes, I can hear with my ears.

What can I do with my eyes that I can NOT do with my ears?

Yes, I can see with my eyes.

(Turn around and laugh.) How do you think I feel?

How can you tell I'm HAPPY?

If a child says, "You're laughing," ask, "How can you tell I'm laughing?" Stay turned around, then ask the following questions:

Can you see my face with your eyes?

Can you hear me laugh? Can you hear me with your ears?

So you can tell I'm HAPPY because you can hear me, but you can NOT see me.

Face the group and laugh again.

Now how can you tell I'm HAPPY?

You can see me with your _____. *(Point to your eyes.)*

AND you can hear me with your _____. *(Point to your ears.)*

Hold up the penny for the group to see.

I have a penny. Can you see the penny?

Yes, you can see the penny with your _____.

Can you hear the penny?

No, you can NOT hear the penny.

So you have two ways now to find out how someone feels. Do you know a third way *(show three fingers)* to find out how someone feels?

Yes, you can ask.

_____, ask me how I feel NOW.

Good, I feel HAPPY. How do you feel?

How did I find out how you feel?

I asked you AND I heard you tell me. I heard you with my _____.
(Point to your ears.)

Happy-Sad: More How Can You Tell?

PURPOSE

To highlight three ways of understanding people's HAPPY and SAD feelings: watching, listening, and asking

MATERIALS

Illustrations 2 and 3

TEACHER SCRIPT

Show children Illustration 2 (happy face).

How do you think this boy is feeling?

How can you tell?

Can you hear him with your ears?

Can you ask him?

Can you see him with your eyes?

Yes, you can see him, but you can NOT hear him or ask him.

Can you ALL make a HAPPY face? Let's make a HAPPY face together.

Can I see your HAPPY face with my eyes?

Can I ask you how you feel?

Now I'm going to ask you.

(Child 1), what makes you feel HAPPY?

Oh, I asked you AND I heard what you said.

(To the group) IF you cry, can I hear that you're HAPPY?

No. What can you do so I can hear that you're HAPPY?

Ask three or four more children what makes them feel happy. You can integrate these questions into the curriculum by pairing them with the concepts left and right. For example:

> (Child 2), turn to the child on your right and ask what makes (him/her) feel HAPPY.
>
> (Child 3), turn to the child on your left and ask the SAME question.

Repeat as time and interest permit. Next show children Illustration 3 (sad face).

> How does this girl feel?
>
> Does she feel the SAME way OR a DIFFERENT way as this boy? *(Point to Illustration 2.)*
>
> How can you tell she's SAD? (*If a child says, "She's crying":* How can you tell she's crying?)
>
> Can you hear her?
>
> Can you ask her?
>
> No, but you can see her with your _____. *(Point to your eyes.)*
>
> Let me see ALL of you make a SAD face.
>
> (Child 4), what makes you feel SAD?
>
> How did I find out what makes you SAD?
>
> Yes, I asked you AND I heard what you said.
>
> *(To the group)* IF you laugh, can I hear that you feel SAD?
>
> No. What can you do so I will hear that you feel SAD?
>
> Yes, you can cry.

Ask three or four more children what makes them feel sad.

ILLUSTRATION 2   Lesson 17

ILLUSTRATION 3   Lesson 17

Angry

PURPOSE

To help children become aware of others' ANGRY feelings, to later avoid negative interpersonal consequences

MATERIALS

Illustrations 2 and 3 (from Lesson 17), Illustration 4 (from this lesson)

TEACHER SCRIPT

Show children Illustrations 2 and 3.

> I can feel _____. *(Indicate happy face.)*
>
> I can feel _____. *(Indicate sad face.)*
>
> There is a third way *(show three fingers)* that I can feel.

Show children Illustration 4 (angry face).

> Do you know how I feel when I look like this?
>
> Yes, ANGRY. ANGRY and mad are the SAME feeling.
>
> *(Point to Illustration 4.)* How does this boy feel?
>
> Does he feel the SAME way OR a DIFFERENT way as this girl? *(Point to Illustration 3.)*
>
> How can you tell he's ANGRY?
>
> Can you hear him with your ears?
>
> Can you see him with your eyes?
>
> *(To the group)* Can you ALL make an ANGRY face?
>
> Can I see you with my eyes?
>
> Can I hear you with my ears?
>
> Can I ask you how you feel?
>
> I have three ways to find out how you feel.

Who can tell me what they are? Way number one is _____.

And number two?

Number three?

_____, what makes you feel ANGRY?

How did I find out what makes you feel ANGRY?

Yes, I asked you.

Ask three or four more children what makes them feel ANGRY.

HINT

You may notice that some children become more emotional as the sequence of games dealing with emotions continues. However, their emotional discomfort is only temporary; once children can think through their emotions, they can usually cope with them better than before.

ILLUSTRATION 4 Lesson 18

Might-Maybe, More How People Feel

PURPOSE

To illustrate people's feelings and show that what we do or say can make them feel HAPPY, SAD, or ANGRY, as well as to introduce the words MIGHT and MAYBE to help children understand that we cannot always know how people feel

MATERIALS

Various classroom objects (for example, books, toys, crayons)

TEACHER SCRIPT

(Child 1), what do you do to look HAPPY?

(Using appropriate voice, to the group) Can you all show me a SAD face?

(Show an angry face.) How do you look when you're ANGRY? Mad and ANGRY are the SAME feeling.

(Child 2), do you like to play with dolls?

(If child responds yes) If someone gave you a doll, how would that make you feel?

Yes, that would probably make you feel HAPPY.

Now let's ALL pretend that (Child 2) has a doll to play with and (Child 3) snatches it away.

How would that make (Child 2) feel?

MAYBE it would make (Child 2) feel ANGRY *(show angry expression)* or SAD *(show sad expression).*

I said MAYBE because MAYBE means we don't know for sure. How can we find out?

Let's ask. (Child 2), if (Child 3) snatched a doll from you, how would that make you feel? *(If needed:* ANGRY or SAD?)

Now here is a new game. I'm going to give each of you something.

Give each child an object, then choose a child who is generally not aggressive to begin the game.

(Child 4), snatch the _____ from (Child 5). Remember, this is just a game!

(Child 5), how do you feel about that?

(Child 4), let (him/her) have it back.

NOW how do you feel, (Child 5)?

Repeat this pattern with other pairs.

(Child 6), how would going for a ride on a pony make you feel?

Let's pretend that someone came and took the pony away, and you could NOT have a ride. How would you feel then?

Now let's pretend the person came back and said, "OK, you can go for a ride." How would that make you feel?

How do you think (Child 7) MIGHT feel if we let (him/her) play with this _____? *(Indicate a classroom object.)*

MAYBE (he/she) would feel HAPPY and MAYBE NOT. Let's find out. How can we find out? *(Encourage children to ask.)*

Let's pretend someone came along and threw the _____ out the window so that (Child 7) could NOT play with it anymore.

NOW how do you think (Child 7) MIGHT feel?

(He/she) MIGHT feel SAD, OR (he/she) MIGHT feel ANGRY. How can we find out? *(Encourage children to ask.)*

(Child 8), take this _____ and give it to (Child 9). *(Indicate another classroom object.)*

Does that make (Child 9) HAPPY? MAYBE yes and MAYBE no.

(Child 9), how could we find out if you like this?

Yes, we could ask you.

Can anybody think of another way to find out if (Child 9) likes this? *(If needed:* You could see Child 9 playing with it. Then you would know.)

Let's pretend that (Child 10) is going to go up the steps of a slide.

Now let's pretend that someone comes along and pushes (him/her) out of the way and goes up first.

How do you think that would make (Child 10) feel?

MAYBE that would make (him/her) feel SAD, OR MAYBE it would make (him/her) feel ANGRY.

How can we find out? *(Encourage children to ask.)*

What would make you feel ANGRY, (Child 11)?

And what would make you feel HAPPY, (Child 11)?

Give each child in the group a chance to share what would make him or her angry and happy.

(*To the group*) What did we learn from all this? (*If needed:* People have feelings, and what we do or say can make them feel HAPPY, SAD, or ANGRY.)

HINT

If a generally responsive child begins to show signs of tension or temporary emotional upset, he may face the other way or even pout. You can ask the group, "Is _____ feeling HAPPY or SAD?" then ask the child, "Why are you feeling (SAD/ANGRY)?" If the child does not answer, you can ask the group, "Can anybody guess why _____ is feeling (SAD/ANGRY)?" If the child continues to pout, ask the group, "Can anyone think of a way to help _____ feel HAPPY again?" Giving attention through participation in the program helps bring the child back to the lesson.

Are You Listening to Me?

PURPOSE

To show children the importance of listening and responding to what someone else is saying

MATERIALS

Any two hand puppets (for example, Ellie the Elephant and Rudy the Rooster)

TEACHER SCRIPT

Teacher: This is Ellie the Elephant. And this is Rudy the Rooster. They are talking to each other. Listen.

Ellie: My knee is bleeding.

Rudy: I like french fries.

Teacher: What's wrong about the way Rudy answered Ellie? Did Rudy listen to Ellie? What MIGHT Rudy say if he really listened to Ellie when Ellie said her knee was bleeding? *(Let children respond.)* Let's try another one.

Ellie: I got a new racing car for my birthday.

Rudy: I wonder whether it will rain today. *(Pauses.)* Oops! I mean, that's nice. I like cars.

Have two children come up and each pretend to be a puppet.

(To the children) Ellie, say something to Rudy.

Rudy, say something that shows you did NOT listen to Ellie.

Ellie, say what you said BEFORE.

Rudy, this time say something that shows you did listen to Ellie.

Continue with new children as time and interest permit.

OK, now listen carefully. Rudy and Ellie are going to talk to each other again.

When Rudy says something that you think shows he IS listening to Ellie, raise your hand.

If you think Rudy says something that shows he is NOT listening to Ellie, just sit still.

Ellie: My knee is bleeding.

Rudy: I like strawberries.

Ellie: I need a bandage.

Rudy: Today's my birthday.

Ellie: My knee really hurts.

Rudy: Why does your knee hurt? *(Children raise hands.)*

Ellie: Because I fell.

Rudy: Oh, you fell. *(Children raise hands.)*

If a child answers inappropriately, ask why he or she thinks that way.

What did we learn from this? (*If needed:* If you're going to talk with someone, it is important to hear with your ears what they say. IF you do NOT really listen and hear what they say, THEN you MIGHT sound very silly.)

A Story

PURPOSE

To help children understand what it is like to listen and feel listened to

MATERIALS

Any storybook that depicts one character not listening to another

TEACHER SCRIPT

Read the story. If necessary, reread. At appropriate points, ask the following questions:

How did (Character 1) feel when no one listened to (him/her)?
What happened when no one listened?

IS (Character 1) a _____? *(Name something the character is not.)*
No, (he/she) is NOT a _____.

(He/she) is NOT a balloon.

Let's be silly. (He/she) is NOT a _____.

(Character 1) _____. *(Describe something the character did.)* Did (he/she) do that BEFORE or AFTER _____? *(Describe an event occurring earlier in the story.)*

Did (Character 1) listen to what (Character 2) said about _____?

IF someone does NOT listen to you, THEN how do you feel about that?

How do you think I feel when no one listens to me?

How do you think (Character 1) felt when (Character 2) _____? *(Describe an event in the story.)*

Why do you think (he/she) felt that way?

Would you feel the SAME way OR a DIFFERENT way as (Character 1) about _____?

Discuss any differences in feelings about any story event.

Finding Out What People Like

PURPOSE

To encourage sensitivity to others' preferences and to strengthen awareness that asking is one way to find out about them

MATERIALS

Illustrations 5–12

TEACHER SCRIPT

Show children any two of the illustrations.

Who can tell us what this is? *(Point to one illustration.)*

Right, a _____. And this? *(Point to the other illustration.)*

(To Child 1) If you could choose a _____ OR a _____, which would you choose? That means you can choose only one.

(To Child 2) Which one would you choose?

(To the group) (Child 1) chose the _____. (Child 2) chose the _____.

Did (Child 1) AND (Child 2) choose the SAME thing OR something DIFFERENT?

Yes, they chose (the SAME thing/something DIFFERENT).

Repeat with other picture pairs and different children. Then show another illustration.

(To Child 3) Would this _____ make you HAPPY?

(To the group) What did I just do to find out?
Yes, I asked.

Let's ALL say together: "Would a _____ make you HAPPY?"

Repeat with other illustrations and different children until someone says no.

Is it OK for DIFFERENT children to like DIFFERENT things?

Yes, it is OK.

HINT

Encourage the shy nonresponder to point to one picture or the other, then ask, "Did you choose a _____ OR a _____? Just tell me _____ OR _____." Even if the child does not respond verbally, at least she has participated by pointing to a picture. Such a child will sometimes respond to another child, if not to you.

ILLUSTRATION 5 Lesson 22

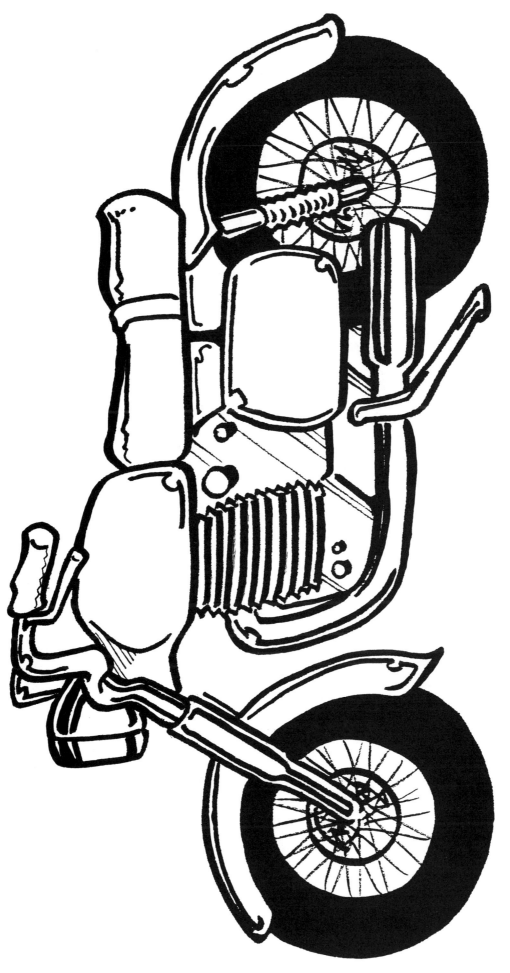

ILLUSTRATION 6   Lesson 22

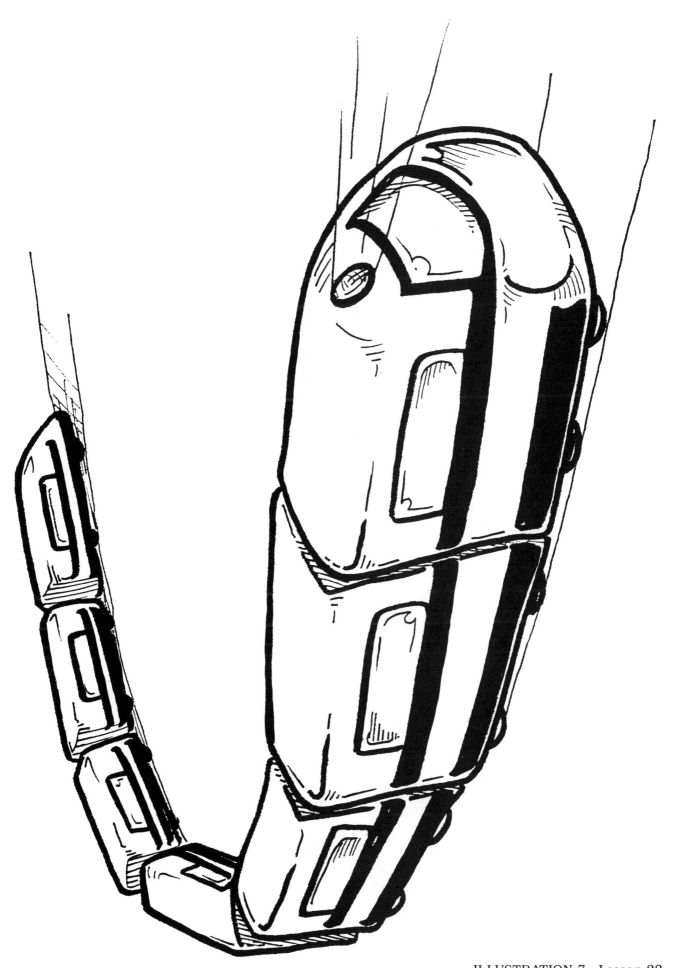

ILLUSTRATION 7 Lesson 22

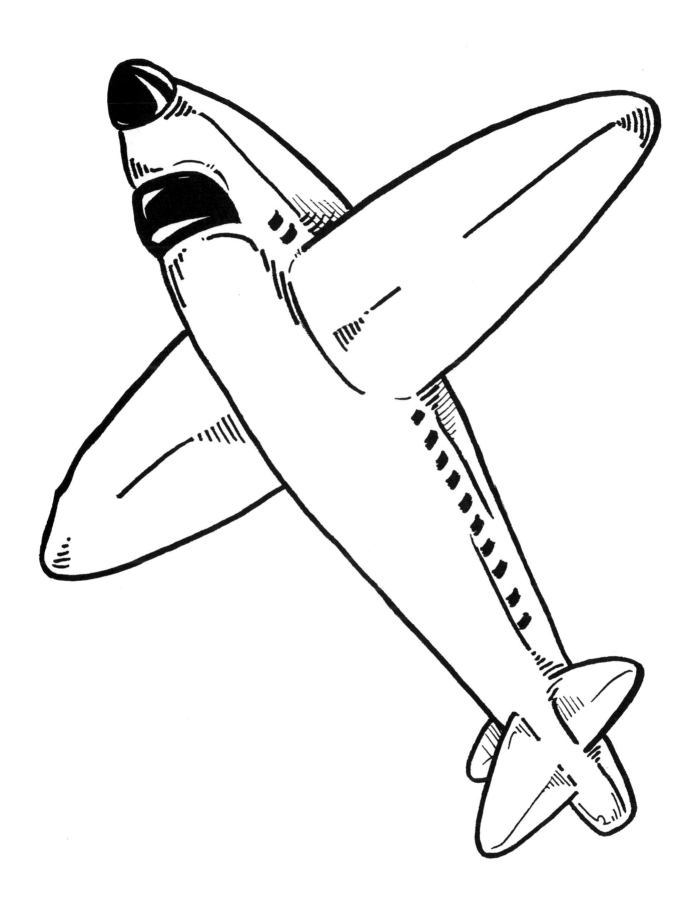

ILLUSTRATION 8   Lesson 22

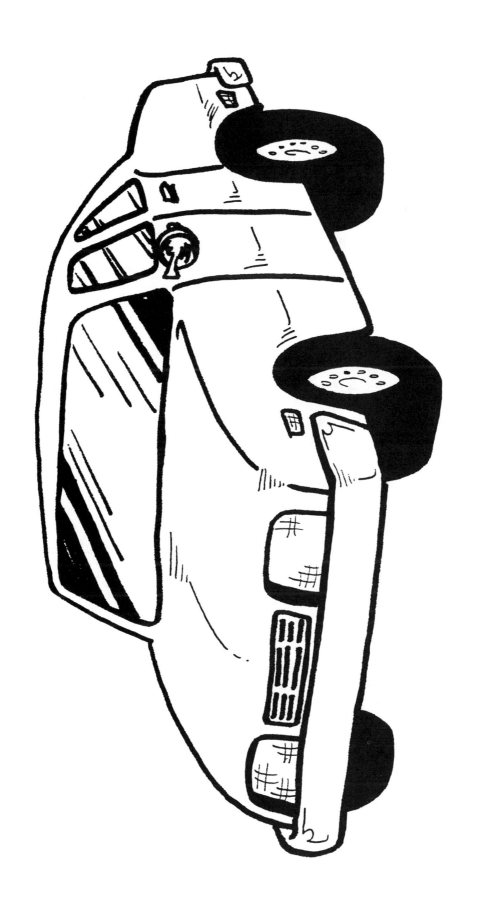

ILLUSTRATION 9   Lesson 22

ILLUSTRATION 10 Lesson 22

ILLUSTRATION 11 Lesson 22

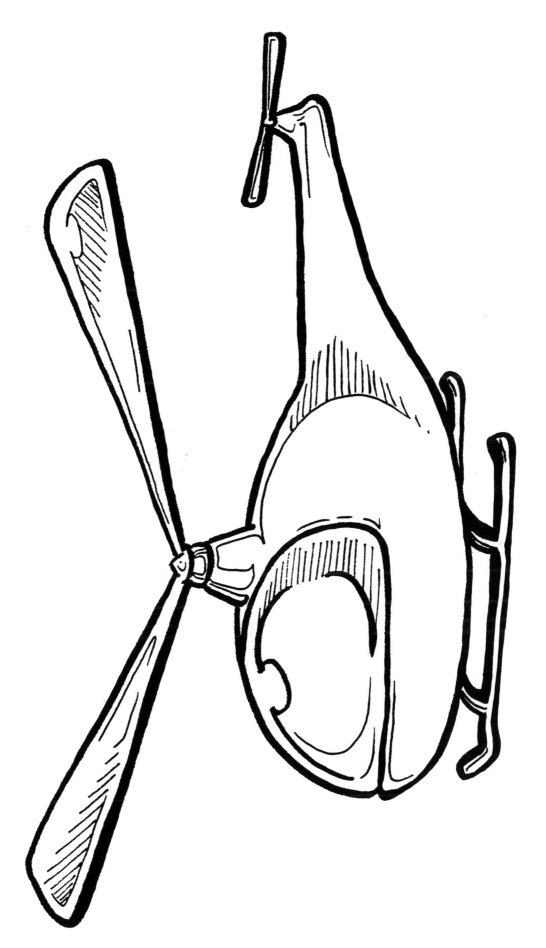

ILLUSTRATION 12   Lesson 22

Do You Like?

PURPOSE

To show children that one way to find out others' preferences is to ask, "Do you like?"

MATERIALS

Illustrations 5–12 (from Lesson 22)

TEACHER SCRIPT

Show children any two of the illustrations.

(Child 1), which picture do you think (Child 2) would choose?

How can you find out? (*If needed:* Go ahead and ask.)

Repeat with other picture pairs and different children.

Now we're going to play a game called Do You Like?

Asking "Do you like?" is one way to find out what makes people HAPPY.

Who can think of a way to make (Child 3) HAPPY?

How can you find out if that would make (him/her) HAPPY? (*If needed:* Go ahead and ask.)

Repeat with two or three children.

(Child 4), do you like to play with trucks?

Do you like hamburgers?

Do you like balloons?

If yes to all three: (Child 4) likes _____ AND _____ AND _____. DIFFERENT things make the SAME child HAPPY.

If no to one or more: (Child 4) likes SOME of these things.

Let children get carried away by asking one another, "Do you like?"

HINT

Having group members ask a shy, nonresponsive child this question can be very useful. When someone names something the child likes, sometimes she will smile, feel part of the group, and begin to respond. If the child has been nonverbal and begins to repeat what another child has said, praise by saying, "Good, you told us, too."

Finding Out About Others' Feelings

LUNCHTIME/JUICETIME

I like (hamburgers).

Do you like the SAME thing OR something DIFFERENT?

Ask several children about their preferences. Point out who likes the same thing and who likes different things.

LISTENING AND PARTICIPATING

If you do NOT listen when I talk to you, how do you think that makes me feel?

Yes, (ANGRY/SAD).

What can you do so I will NOT feel (ANGRY/SAD)?

Did I feel (ANGRY/SAD) BEFORE or AFTER you stopped listening to me?

Will I feel (ANGRY/SAD) AFTER you start listening to me again?

How does Ellie the Elephant feel when Rudy the Rooster does NOT listen to her?

How do you think I feel when you do NOT listen to me?

If someone is NOT listening, how can I tell?

What can you say so I know you are listening to me?

IF you do NOT get your work done on time, THEN how will you feel about that?

TRANSITIONS

IF you disrupt our line, THEN how will I feel about that?

IF others have to wait for you to get into line, THEN they will be late to (gym). How MIGHT they feel about that?

OTHER INTERACTIONS

How does _____ feel?

How can you tell?

You can see (him/her) with your _____. *(Point dramatically to your eyes.)*

AND you can hear (him/her) with your _____. *(Point dramatically to your ears.)*

Do you know why _____ is (HAPPY/SAD/ANGRY)?

How can you find out?

If needed: Go ahead and ask.

If sad or angry: Can you think of a way to help _____ feel HAPPY again?

After child responds: Go ahead and try that.

If unsuccessful: Oh, you'll have to think of something DIFFERENT. Can you remember the Do You Like Game?

Try using the following sequence when you are angry because of a child's behavior.

I feel ANGRY NOW.

Do you know why?

What did you (or the class) do or say that made me feel ANGRY?

Can you think of something you can do or say so I will NOT feel ANGRY?

Do you know why I feel ANGRY when:

- You do NOT listen?
- You throw food?
- You interrupt me?

Try using the following sequence when you are angry about something unrelated to a child's behavior.

I feel ANGRY NOW.

I MIGHT NOT feel ANGRY LATER.

Can you think of something to do until LATER, when I can talk to you (or am in a better mood)?

MINI-DIALOGUE

Notice how the teacher in this example asks what happened but avoids reacting to outcomes. Instead, the teacher is sensitive to the children's feelings and helps them come up with a solution to the problem as they see it.

Situation: Two children are fighting.

Teacher: *(To Child 1)* What happened? What's the matter?

Child 1: He hit me.

Teacher: *(To Child 2)* What do you think happened?

Child 2: He broke the red crayon in two.

Teacher: Do you two see what happened the SAME way OR a DIFFERENT way?

Child 1: A DIFFERENT way.

Teacher: Oh, that means we have a problem. *(To Child 1)* How did you feel when (Child 2) did that?

Child 1: ANGRY.

Teacher: *(To Child 2)* How did you feel when that happened?

Child 2: ANGRY.

Teacher: Can either of you think of a way to solve the problem? That means to make it so you'll both feel better.

Child 1: NOT fight.

Teacher: That's *one* way. *(To Child 2)* Can you think of a DIFFERENT way?

Child 2: Be friends.

Teacher: What can you do to show (Child 1) that you want to be friends?

Child 2: *(Shakes Child 1's hand.)*

Teacher: You both thought of a way. You thought of them all by yourselves. How does that make you feel?

Child 1: HAPPY.

Finding Out About Others' Feelings

NEWS AND EVENTS OF THE DAY

How do you feel when your team wins the game?

How do you feel when your team loses?

Did anything happen to you today that made you feel (HAPPY/SAD/ANGRY)?

Turn to the child on your right and find out how (he/she) feels today.
Find out why.

Turn to the child on your left and do the SAME thing.

How do you feel about _____? *(Describe any news item that the children are aware of.)*

Why do you feel that way?

READING AND STORY COMPREHENSION

How did the (boy) in the story I just read feel when (his sister yelled at him)?

MATH

Would you feel HAPPIER if you had a whole pizza OR a half a pizza? *(Repeat with a third, an eighth, and so on.)*

Who would NOT feel HAPPIER with a whole pizza?

Do ALL of you feel the SAME way about pizza, OR do SOME of you feel a DIFFERENT way?

How would your baseball team feel if they had 3 runs and the other team had 6 runs?

SOCIAL STUDIES

How do the people in your neighborhood feel when:

Someone has a block party?

It's clean-the-street day?

Someone is selling drugs?

A house is on fire?

People are fighting?

How can you tell:

If your (dog/cat/bird) is HAPPY, SAD, or ANGRY? Any other way?

That popcorn is being popped? Any other way?

That someone is chewing gum? Any other way?

How do you feel about:

People throwing food and other garbage into the streets? Any other feelings?

Whales that get trapped or fish that get poisoned by chemicals? Any other feelings?

MUSIC

How does music make you feel?

Who does NOT like music?

Does music make ALL of you or SOME of you feel HAPPY?

Do You Remember? Part I

PURPOSE

To form the basis for later remembering things about people and to strengthen ability to pay attention

MATERIALS

Illustrations 5–12 (from Lesson 22) or pictures of different animals, cut from magazines and pasted on posterboard

TEACHER SCRIPT

Show children any six of the illustrations. Ask three children to come to the front to choose one.

(Child 1), pick one picture that you like—just one.

OK, stand up here and show it to the class.

(Child 2), now you choose one picture and show it to the class.

(Child 3), now you choose.

(To the group) What does (Child 1) like?

What does (Child 2) like?

What does (Child 3) like?

Look carefully. You will have to remember what each child has.

Ask the children in the front to turn their pictures around so that they are not visible.

Who can remember what (Child 1) likes?

Who can remember what (Child 2) likes?

Who can remember what (Child 3) likes?

After the group makes a guess for each child, ask the child to turn the picture around so the group can see it. To make the task harder, you may wish to increase the number of children in front or give some children two pictures.

Do You Remember? Part II

PURPOSE

To strengthen children's ability to remember things about people and to reinforce listening and paying attention

MATERIALS

Chalkboard or easel (for Variation 2)

TEACHER SCRIPT

Variation 1

Today's ICPS game is about what people do to make you feel DIFFERENT ways.

First, I'm going to ask some of you to tell us what your friend MIGHT do to make you feel HAPPY.

Listen very carefully because you will have to remember what each child says.

Have three children stand at the front of the group.

(Child 1), what does your friend do that makes you feel HAPPY?

(Child 2), what does your friend do that makes you feel HAPPY?

(Child 3), what does your friend do that makes you feel HAPPY?

Who can remember what (Child 1) said?

What (Child 2) said?

How about (Child 3)?

Keep adding children at the front of the group as far as the group can be challenged.

Variation 2

Call three children to the front, as for Variation 1. Divide the remaining children into teams, then see which team can remember more of the children's responses. Tally points on the chalkboard.

> (Child 1), what does your friend do that makes you feel HAPPY?
>
> (Child 2), what does your friend do that makes you feel HAPPY?
>
> (Child 3), what does your friend do that makes you feel HAPPY?

Ask each team the following types of questions. Continue as long as children are able to give answers.

> Who can tell us what each child said?
>
> Who said (candy) makes (him/her) HAPPY?
>
> What did (Child 1) say makes (him/her) HAPPY?
>
> What did (Child 2) AND (Child 3) say makes them HAPPY?
>
> Who did NOT say (pizza) makes them HAPPY?

Variation 3

Ask children the following sets of questions, then have them stand in three separate locations on the basis of their answers. Continue the questioning until everyone is in one of the groups.

> Who feels HAPPY today?
>
> Why do you feel HAPPY today?
>
> OK, you come stand over here.

> Who feels SAD today?
>
> Why do you feel SAD today?
>
> You stand over here.

> And who feels ANGRY?
>
> Why do you feel ANGRY today?
>
> OK, you stand over here.

> Now I'm going to mix everybody up.
>
> Look carefully to see who is in each group because you will have to remember who belongs in which group.

Mix the groups up.

> Who is in the SAD group NOW but was in the HAPPY group BEFORE?

> Who is in the ANGRY group NOW but was in the HAPPY group BEFORE?

> Ask everybody to return to the original groups.

> Does anyone in the SAD or ANGRY group want to be in the HAPPY group?

> Who can think of a way to make _____ feel HAPPY?

> How can you find out? (*If needed:* Go ahead and ask.)

When something is suggested that would make the child happy, he or she may move to the happy group. Repeat until all who want to be in the happy group have moved there.

More Might-Maybe, Why-Because

PURPOSE

To encourage preliminary understanding of the connection between an act and its consequence and to promote awareness that consequences are never a certainty

MATERIALS

Any hand puppet (for example, Kookie the Crow)

TEACHER SCRIPT

Today's ICPS game starts with more about the words MIGHT and MAYBE.

I like to dance.

I do NOT know if you like to dance.

MAYBE you do, and MAYBE you do NOT.

Remember when we played the Do You Like Game?

In that game, we had to find out what people like.

Remember, MAYBE means there is no way to know for sure.

(To Child 1) Do you like to dance? *(Let child respond.)*

How did I find out? *(If needed:* I asked.)

Repeat with three or four more children.

IF I snatched the toy that (Child 2) is playing with, THEN how do you think (he/she) would feel? *(Let children respond.)*

(Child 2) MIGHT feel that way.

How can we find out? *(If needed:* We can ask.)

Repeat with three or four more children, then put the puppet on your hand and present the following exchange.

Kookie:	I'm Kookie the Crow! I came to play a game with you today. I came to play the WHY-BECAUSE game. Let me show you how to play. First I'll play with your teacher. *(Pauses.)* Teacher, I'm very tired.
Teacher:	WHY?
Kookie:	BECAUSE I forgot to take my nap. *(To the group)* Now I'm going to play with you. When I say something, ask me "WHY?" real loud, OK? Let's try it. *(Pauses.)* I'm very hungry.
Children:	WHY?
Kookie:	BECAUSE I haven't had my lunch. *(Pauses.)* I like going to school.
Children:	WHY?
Kookie:	BECAUSE the children are my friends. *(Pauses.)* I can't sing today.
Children:	WHY?
Kookie:	BECAUSE my throat hurts. *(Pauses.)* Now let's change the game. I'm going to ask you "WHY?" and you make up the BECAUSE. Now listen. *(To the teacher)* I am going to the store. I am going to walk. I am NOT going to take the bus. Can you guess WHY I'm going to walk?
Teacher:	BECAUSE your friend is walking to the store and you want to walk with your friend?
Kookie:	MAYBE. Can you think of a DIFFERENT BECAUSE?
Teacher:	BECAUSE it's a nice day out?
Kookie:	*(To the group)* See, there is more than one BECAUSE. Now let's play together. *(Pauses.)* Johnny won't come to my house and play with me today. WHY won't Johnny come to my house and play with me today? Does anybody have a BECAUSE?
Children:	*(Respond.)*
Kookie:	MAYBE he won't come BECAUSE _____. *(Repeats the response.)* Does anybody have a DIFFERENT BECAUSE?

Continue until children run out of responses.

Kookie: Let's play this game again. *(Pauses.)* I like birthday parties. Can you guess WHY I like birthday parties?

Children: *(Respond.)*

Kookie: Very good. MAYBE I like birthday parties BECAUSE _____.
Now let's think of a DIFFERENT BECAUSE. I like birthday parties BECAUSE _____.

Continue until children run out of responses.

Teacher: OK, very good! WHY does Kookie like birthday parties?
MAYBE it's BECAUSE _____ OR BECAUSE _____
OR BECAUSE _____. *(Repeat children's answers in the order given.)*

Repeat this line of questioning by asking, about an absent child, "WHY is _____ NOT here today?"

HINT

If a child is running around or in other ways disrupting the group, say, in a normal, nonthreatening tone of voice, "_____, WHY are you doing something DIFFERENT?" If the child does not answer, ask others in the group why they think the child is being disruptive.

Afraid

PURPOSE

To help children understand the meaning of the word AFRAID, as well as to increase awareness of other feeling words

MATERIALS

None

TEACHER SCRIPT

Some kids, if they see a monster, get scared or AFRAID.

Scared and AFRAID are the SAME feeling.

What else MIGHT make someone feel AFRAID? (*If needed:* Would some kids be scared if they were alone in the dark? If someone made a loud noise?)

Does anything make you feel AFRAID?

What makes you feel ANGRY?

How about HAPPY?

SAD?

Discuss as time and interest permit.

HINT

An extremely verbal child may consistently be the first to respond; give long, drawn-out responses; and in general dominate the group. To avoid losing the interest of such a child, you can say, "You have just had a long turn. Now a DIFFERENT child needs a turn." You can then encourage the dominating child to pick someone who has not had a turn. Using ICPS style prevents the child from feeling frustrated and potentially withdrawing or engaging in disruptive behaviors.

Let's Make Up a Story, Part I

PURPOSE

To encourage story comprehension and increase sensitivity to feelings

MATERIALS

Chalkboard or easel

TEACHER SCRIPT

Read the beginning of the following story to the group, inviting them to fill in the missing information.

Joan and Robert were riding a bike together.

They felt very _____.

Then Nancy came and started to make Joan ANGRY.

Nancy made Joan ANGRY BECAUSE _____.

Well, the bike was very old.

When Joan and Robert started to ride it again, the wheel came flying off.

Joan and Robert started to cry.

They felt very _____.

Nancy loved to tease Joan and Robert.

When Nancy saw the wheel come off, she laughed.

She said, "I'm glad your old wheel came off. Ha, Ha, Ha."

Joan and Robert felt _____.

Joan and Robert looked at Nancy and made Nancy AFRAID BECAUSE _____.

What happens next in this story? You make it up.

Write the story on the chalkboard as it unfolds.

Let's Make Up a Story, Part II

PURPOSE

To encourage story comprehension and show children that people can feel DIFFERENT ways about the SAME thing

MATERIALS

None

TEACHER SCRIPT

We're going to make up a story together, and we're going to have in our story the words HAPPY and AFRAID.

Scared and AFRAID are the SAME feeling.

Who can tell us something that makes you feel AFRAID?
(Let children respond.)

Read the following story to the group, inviting them to fill in the missing information.

Shawn just got a new basketball for his birthday.

James got a new basketball, too.

Shawn was playing with his new basketball, and some other kids saw him and asked him to play with them.

Shawn felt very HAPPY about that. He felt HAPPY about that BECAUSE _____.

LATER in the day the kids saw James with his new basketball, and they asked him to play with them.

But James felt AFRAID.

MAYBE James felt AFRAID BECAUSE _____.

Did Shawn and James feel the SAME way OR a DIFFERENT way about playing basketball with the other kids?

Test children's story comprehension by asking them the following questions:

Did Shawn get a new basketball or a new football?

Did he get his new basketball for his birthday or for Christmas?

Who felt HAPPY about playing with the other kids, Shawn or James?

WHY did Shawn feel HAPPY? *(Accept any reason previously given.)*

How did James feel about that? WHY?

Did the kids see Shawn BEFORE or AFTER they saw James?

Now let's think of something new. The SAME child can come to feel a DIFFERENT way about the SAME thing.

Continue with the story.

James felt AFRAID.

MAYBE it was BECAUSE he did NOT know how to shoot baskets, and he thought the kids would laugh at him and tease him.

Then a friend came over and showed James how to shoot baskets.

James got very good at it.

He shot two *(show two fingers)* baskets, then three *(show three fingers),* then how many?

Yes, four.

NOW how do you think James felt?

How did James feel BEFORE he could shoot baskets?

How did he feel AFTER he could shoot baskets?

What did we learn about this? *(If needed:* We learned that the SAME child can feel DIFFERENT ways about the SAME thing. First James felt AFRAID. Then he felt _____.)

Can you think of something that used to make you feel AFRAID but that doesn't anymore?

WHY are you not AFRAID of that NOW?

My ICPS Book, Part I

PURPOSE

To help children understand and express their feelings by drawing them

MATERIALS

Chalkboard or easel

Paper and crayons

A folder for each child

Feeling face stickers

TEACHER SCRIPT

> **NOTE**
>
> For feeling face stickers, duplicate the drawings provided, then cut them out or have children cut them out. Put a piece of double-stick tape on the back of each face. Approximately 6 feeling face stickers of each type (a total of 24) will be needed per child for the entire program. Alternatively, children may draw the faces. If you wish, you may place extra feeling face stickers in a basket. Children can pick one to wear during the day when they want to express how they feel about something.

Today we're going to do something DIFFERENT.

We're going to start our ICPS books.

Do you remember what ICPS means? (*If needed:* I Can Problem Solve.)

I want you to draw something you did today, something that happened to you, or anything you can think of that made you feel HAPPY, SAD, ANGRY, or AFRAID.

After the children have finished their drawings:

Now I want you to pick out a feeling sticker (or draw the face) that shows how you feel about what you drew in your picture.

Next ask children to tell you about their drawings and the feeling faces they used. Write the feeling words on the chalkboard. If children can print, have them copy the appropriate feeling word from the board onto their drawings. If time permits, you or the children can write down what made them feel this way, as the sample drawing, done by a 6-year-old, shows. Save the children's drawing in their individual ICPS folders.

HINT

Drawing is especially helpful for inhibited children who are not yet ready to verbalize feelings.

SAMPLE DRAWING: FEELINGS

I am sad

My toy airplane almost blew my hair off.

Dilly the Duck, Part I

PURPOSE

To show children how feelings can change and to help them cope with their feelings

MATERIALS

Any two hand puppets (for example, Dilly the Duck and Poppy the Pup)

TEACHER SCRIPT

Dilly: I am Dilly the Duck. I have little, tiny legs. I can NOT run and play with my friends. I wish I could run and play with my friends.

Teacher: *(With a sad voice, turning Dilly's head down)* How does Dilly feel NOW? *(Let children respond.)* WHY does he feel SAD? BECAUSE _____. Well, one day Poppy the Pup came and saw Dilly crying.

Poppy: Dilly, WHY are you so SAD?

Dilly: BECAUSE I can't run and play with my friends.

Poppy: But you can swim. You can swim faster than all the other ducks. All the other ducks want you to play with them. They like you very much.

Dilly: *(Opens mouth wide.)*

Teacher: How does Dilly feel NOW? *(Let children respond.)*

Yes, he feels HAPPY. How did he feel BEFORE? *(Pull Dilly's head down and mouth in. Let children respond.)*

See, BEFORE, he was SAD. *(Pull Dilly's head up and open mouth wide.)*

NOW he is HAPPY. He feels DIFFERENT. He swam with the other ducks, and he showed them all how to swim very fast. *(Demonstrate swimming motion.)*

You know what? While he was swimming, Dilly found out he could do some new tricks. He could do a somersault in the water. *(Demonstrate.)* He found that he could twist and turn in the water. *(Demonstrate.)*

Dilly the Duck, Part II

PURPOSE

To show children that it is possible to like DIFFERENT things at DIFFERENT times and to emphasize that finding out what others like is helpful in problem solving

MATERIALS

Any two hand puppets (for example, Dilly the Duck and Poppy the Pup)

TEACHER SCRIPT

Hide Poppy the Pup behind your back or under the table.

Teacher: Here's Dilly the Duck again. Remember when we found out that Dilly loves to swim and learn new tricks? How did he feel when he was swimming yesterday? *(Let children respond.)*

Yes, he felt HAPPY BECAUSE he loves to swim, and he's a very fast swimmer, too.

Dilly: I've been swimming all morning. This morning some of my friends asked me to swim with them, and I said yes. They know I love to swim.

With Dilly on one hand, bring Poppy the Pup in slowly on the other.

Dilly: Here comes one of my friends, Poppy the Pup! She loves to swim, too.

Poppy: Hi, Dilly. We sure had fun swimming this morning. We both love to swim, don't we? Let's go swimming again now. That would make me very HAPPY.

Dilly: *(Pulls in mouth and turns head down.)*

Poppy: What's the matter, Dilly? WHY do you look so SAD? I thought it would make you HAPPY if I asked you to swim.

Dilly: I was HAPPY when we swam this morning. We swam for a long time. I would NOT be HAPPY to swim again this afternoon.

Poppy: *(To the group)* I guess he doesn't want to play with me. I'll have to think of something so he'll want to play with me. Oh! I know what I'll do. *(Head down, then to Dilly, excitedly)* Dilly, if you don't want to swim right now, do you want to play with my new ball?

Dilly: No, I don't like that game.

Poppy: *(Head down, then to Dilly, excitedly)* Would you like to find some food to eat?

Dilly: Not NOW. I just ate, and I'm NOT hungry.

Poppy: *(To the group)* I'm going to ask a DIFFERENT question. *(To Dilly)* Dilly, I really want to do something with you. What would you like to do?

Dilly: I'd like to play hide-and-seek.

Poppy: OK, I'd like that, too. I'm glad I asked you. I thought MAYBE you didn't want to play with me.

Dilly: Oh, no. I like you. I just didn't want to swim BECAUSE I wanted to do something DIFFERENT. MAYBE tomorrow we can swim again. MAYBE tomorrow I will want to swim again.

Poppy: OK, let's play hide-and-seek now.

Hide Dilly behind your back and have Poppy find him.

Teacher: Dilly and Poppy played hide-and-seek for a while and were very HAPPY. The next day they went swimming again.

Dilly: *(To the group)* Do I like to swim ALL of the time? *(Let children respond.)*

No, sometimes I like to swim, and sometimes I do NOT like to swim. If I swim too much, I MIGHT get tired.

(Child 1), what do you like to do? *(Let child respond.)*

Do you like to _____ ALL of the time or SOME of the time? I bet you'd get tired if you did that ALL of the time.

Let a child come up, hold Dilly, and ask another child, "What do you like to do?" The first child can then ask the second, "Do you like to do that ALL of the time or SOME of the time?"

HINT

For a consistent nonresponder, have Dilly ask, "What do you like to do?" If the child responds, Dilly can ask, "Do you like to do that ALL of the time or SOME of the time?" Or you could let the child pretend to be the puppet, then respond to your question: "Dilly, what do you like to do?" If needed, you can ask a yes-or-no question such as "Do you like to swim?" The extreme nonresponder can hold the puppet and be encouraged to open and close its mouth while you ask these questions. Often such children will begin to talk as the puppet and then, slowly, as themselves.

For a child who exhibits dominating behavior, try the following reminder: "If you talk ALL the time, then other children can NOT have a turn to say what they want to say."

Using the Dilly the Duck Story

MINI-DIALOGUES

The following examples show how the teacher can help children apply their understanding of SOME-ALL concepts to avoid frustration.

Situation 1: Tyrone wants to go outside, but the rest of the class is having storytime.

Tyrone: I want to go outside.

Teacher: Do you remember what Dilly likes to do?

Tyrone: Swim.

Teacher: Does Dilly like to swim SOME of the time or ALL of the time?

Tyrone: SOME of the time.

Teacher: Do you like to go outside SOME of the time or ALL of the time?

If the child says, "All of the time," just say, "I know you're teasing me." This sequence of questions also works well with a child who wants something that is prohibited.

Situation 2: Rico is sad.

Teacher: What's the matter? How are you feeling?

Rico: SAD.

Teacher: Do you feel SAD ALL of the time or SOME of the time?

Rico: SOME of the time.

Teacher: You can feel DIFFERENT ways at DIFFERENT times.

Situation 3: Sandra refuses Beth's request to play.

Beth: No one will play with me.

Teacher: Do you know WHY?

Beth: No!

Teacher: Did Sandra play with you BEFORE?

Beth: Yes.

Teacher: Do you like to play with Sandra SOME of the time or ALL of the time?

Beth: SOME of the time.

Teacher: Does Sandra like to play with you SOME of the time or ALL of the time?

Situation 4: Laura thinks Tammy doesn't want to play with her.

Laura: Tammy, let's jump rope.

Tammy: I don't want to.

Laura: Please.

Tammy: No! I hate jump rope.

Laura: Teacher, no one will play with me.

Teacher: Laura, do you want to play with Tammy OR do you want to jump rope?

Laura: I want to play with Tammy.

Teacher: How can you find out what Tammy likes to do?

Laura: Ask her.

Teacher: Go ahead and ask her.

Laura: Tammy, do you like the dollhouse?

Tammy: Yes.

Laura: You be the mother, and I'll be the baby.

Tammy: OK.

Laura: *(Excitedly sets up the doll house.)*

Here Laura made a quick and faulty assumption. Tammy did want to play with her. She just wanted to do something different from jumping rope. Sometimes a child needs to be helped to identify the problem. In this example, concepts from the Do You Like Game (see Lesson 23) helped.

Proud

PURPOSE

To help children identify this feeling, important in reinforcing themselves for problem solving and other jobs well done

MATERIALS

None

TEACHER SCRIPT

So far we've talked about four words that tell how people feel about things. Do you remember what they are?

Yes, HAPPY, SAD, ANGRY, and AFRAID.

Today's ICPS game is about a new word that tells how people feel about things.

Our new word is PROUD.

PROUD is when someone feels good about something he or she did.

(Make a proud face.) I feel PROUD.

OK. PROUD is when someone feels good about something he or she did:

I cooked a very delicious chicken. I feel PROUD.

A girl I know ran a race and won it. She felt very PROUD.

I drew a picture I liked a lot. That made me feel PROUD.

What makes you feel PROUD of yourself?

Let four or five children answer.

You can also feel PROUD of someone else:

I feel PROUD of you when you try very hard to do something well.

I feel PROUD of you when you try to do well on your math in school.

As long as you try, I feel PROUD.

I also feel PROUD of you when you tell me the truth about something.

I feel PROUD of you when you solve a problem by yourself.

Frustrated

PURPOSE

To help children learn to identify and cope with this feeling, important for later problem solving

MATERIALS

None

TEACHER SCRIPT

NOTE

The feeling word concept FRUSTRATED, as well as the concepts IMPATIENT (Lesson 43) and WORRIED-RELIEVED (Lesson 46), may be too advanced for some kindergartners. If so, these lessons may be omitted.

Today's ICPS feeling word is FRUSTRATED.

That's a big word. Can you say FRUSTRATED?

FRUSTRATED is when things just don't go right.

Things just don't go the way you want them to.

When you want something you can NOT have, you feel FRUSTRATED.

MAYBE you want a toy, and someone won't give it to you.

Has that ever happened to you?

Tell us about it.

How did that make you feel? (*If angry:* ANGRY and _____. What's our big new word?)

MAYBE you want to talk to someone, and the person is busy.

Has that ever happened to you?

Tell us about it.

How did that make you feel?

MAYBE you want to watch television, but your mother says you have to go to bed.

Has that ever happened to you?

Tell us about it.

How did that make you feel?

Is there anything else you wanted and could not have that you would like to tell us about?

You can also feel FRUSTRATED when you try to do something and you can't.

MAYBE you're trying to tie your shoes, and your shoelace breaks.

MAYBE you're trying to skate and you just keep falling.

Has anything like these things ever happened to you?

Tell us about them.

How did they make you feel?

MAYBE you tried to solve a problem between you and your friend, and you just couldn't do it.

Tell us about it.

How did that make you feel?

Is there anything else you tried to do and could NOT do?

Tell us about it and how you felt.

HINT

Throughout this lesson, if needed, ask, "What's our big new feeling word?"

ICPS Words: Proud, Frustrated

When a child is dressing to go outside:

You can tie your own shoelaces. (*Or:* Put on your own boots, button your coat.)

How does that make you feel?

Yes, PROUD.

And I feel PROUD of you, too.

When a child is watching television or a videotape:

Look, (Rudy) is (skating) really well.

How do you think she MIGHT feel?

Yes, PROUD.

Look, (Rudy's) trying to (tie her shoelace) and can't.

How do you think she feels?

Yes, FRUSTRATED.

When a child is doing homework:

When you do ALL your homework, how does that make you feel?

Yes, PROUD.

And I feel PROUD of you, too.

How do you feel when you do a good job on your homework?

Yes, PROUD.

And I feel PROUD of you, too.

I know you are trying to solve this (math) problem, and you find it hard.

I understand you must feel _____.

Yes, FRUSTRATED.

But I know you are trying. That makes me feel _____.

Yes, PROUD.

When a child is attempting to solve problems:

You told me the truth about what happened, and that makes me feel _____.

Yes, I feel PROUD of you.

You tried to solve that problem all by yourself, and that makes me feel _____.

Yes, I feel PROUD of you.

I see you're trying to solve that problem with (Sarah), and I know you feel _____.

Yes, FRUSTRATED.

I bet if you try really hard you can think of one more way.

When a child is trying hard at any task:

Good, you tried hard to _____, and I feel PROUD of you.

How do you feel about yourself when you try hard?

I see you are trying very hard to _____.

I understand you feel FRUSTRATED.

I'm PROUD of you for trying.

When a child is interrupting:

I know you want to talk to me NOW, but I can NOT talk to you NOW.

I understand that makes you feel _____.

Yes, FRUSTRATED.

During school lessons:

When you have your hand up and you want to answer a question, you may feel FRUSTRATED if I do NOT call on you.

Can I call on ALL of you to answer ALL my questions?

No, I can only call on SOME of you.

Do you know WHY I can NOT call on ALL of you?

SOME of you I can call on NOW, and SOME I can call on LATER.

When a group of children are all talking at once:

When you ALL talk at the same time, can I hear you with my ears?

No, I can NOT hear you with my ears.

How do I feel when you ALL talk at the SAME time? (*If angry:* Yes, ANGRY and _____. What's our big new feeling word? Yes, FRUSTRATED.)

At any time:

You're all (standing in line) so nicely.

How do you feel about yourselves?

Yes, PROUD.

And I feel PROUD of you, too.

A Good Time or Not a Good Time? Part I

PURPOSE

To help children learn that timing is an important ingredient in successful problem solving

MATERIALS

Any two hand puppets (for example, Ellie the Elephant and Rudy the Rooster)

Illustration 13

Chalkboard or easel

TEACHER SCRIPT

Today's ICPS lesson is about good times and NOT good times to do things.

This is just pretend, OK?

Oh, I have such a big headache. My head really hurts, and I'm so busy trying to write my lessons on the chalkboard.

Write on the board, holding your head as though it really hurts. Have the puppets ready to begin talking to you.

Ellie:	Teacher, can I go to my brother's room and give him my football?
Teacher:	No, Ellie, I'm very FRUSTRATED, my head really hurts, and I'm very busy. I can't deal with that right now.
Ellie:	*(Goes away, looking sad and frustrated.)*
Teacher:	*(Smiling)* Oh, my headache went away, and I put all my lessons on the board. I feel very good now.
Rudy:	Teacher, can I go to my brother's room and give him my football?
Teacher:	If you are finished with your math, Rudy, you may go.

(To the group) Who picked a better time to tell a problem to the teacher, Ellie or Rudy?

WHY?

Can the SAME person feel DIFFERENT ways at DIFFERENT times?

Who felt a DIFFERENT way at a DIFFERENT time in this story?

Can you think of a time when it was better to wait BEFORE asking someone for something?

Let's pretend your friend just started playing with a toy, and you want that toy.

If your friend has NOT finished a turn, is it a good time or NOT a good time to ask for the toy?

Show children Illustration 13.

See this picture.

What's happening in this picture? (*If needed:* What are these kids doing?)

Is this a good time or NOT a good time for these kids to be talking?

How does the teacher feel about this?

What can these kids do so the teacher will NOT be ANGRY or FRUSTRATED?

When IS a good time for these kids to talk to each other?

When else IS a good time?

ILLUSTRATION 13   Lesson 35

A Good Time or Not a Good Time? Part II

PURPOSE

To strengthen awareness of others' likely feelings about what IS or is NOT a good time for something

MATERIALS

Any two hand puppets (for example, Dilly the Duck and Poppy the Pup)

TEACHER SCRIPT

Dilly: *(To a child in the group)* Hi, _____. Do you want to go to a movie?

Child: *(Responds.)*

Poppy: Hi, Dilly. Want to play with me?

Dilly: *(Keeps talking to the child.)* Let's go to a movie. What movie...

Poppy: *(Interrupts.)* Dilly, please play with me NOW.

Dilly: Poppy, can I talk to you AND to my friend at the SAME time?

Poppy: *(Sadly)* No.

Dilly: Poppy, does that mean this IS or is NOT a good time to talk to me?

Poppy: NOT a good time.

Dilly: How do you think my friend and I feel when you interrupt us?

Poppy: ANGRY.

Dilly: ANGRY AND _____.

Poppy: FRUSTRATED.

Dilly: I know you feel FRUSTRATED, too. But you have to wait until AFTER I'm finished talking to my friend. *(To the child)* Hi again, _____. So when are we going to the movie?

Child: *(Responds.)*

Dilly: OK, let's have lunch first. What do you like to eat?

Child: *(Responds.)*

Dilly: Oh, I like hamburgers and french fries. What television show do you like to watch?

Child: *(Responds.)*

Dilly: I like that show, too. *(To Poppy)* Poppy, you waited very well. I'm PROUD of you. Now I can listen to what you want to tell me.

Poppy: I want to play with you.

Dilly: OK, I will. Is this a good time to ask me?

Poppy: Yes.

Dilly: Was it a good time to ask me to play BEFORE I finished talking to my friend?

Poppy: No, AFTER.

Dilly: Good, I am not ANGRY now.

Let two children play the parts of Dilly and Poppy, devising their own situation to show a good time and not a good time to ask for something.

A Good Time, Not a Good Time

When a child interrupts:

Can I talk to you AND _____ at the SAME time?

If you talk to me while I'm talking to someone else, I feel _____.
What's our big new feeling word? (*If needed:* FRUSTRATED.)

If I am talking to someone, is that a good time or NOT a good time
to try to talk to me?

When IS a good time?

Can you think of something DIFFERENT to do until I can talk
to you?

When a child who was not called on answers:

If I did NOT call on you and you know the answer, I know you feel
_____. (*If needed:* FRUSTRATED.)

But I can NOT call on two people at the SAME time.

When I call on someone else, is that a good time or NOT a good time
to shout out an answer?

When a child is talking to others during a lesson:

(Child 1), can you talk to (Child 2) AND listen to the lesson at
the SAME time?

Is during a lesson a good time or NOT a good time to talk?

When IS a good time to talk?

Puppet Story: Robbie and Poppy

PURPOSE

To emphasize the ideas that it is possible for DIFFERENT people to like DIFFERENT things (to help avoid false conclusions) and that finding out what others like is helpful in problem solving

MATERIALS

Any two hand puppets (for example, Robbie the Rabbit and Poppy the Pup)

TEACHER SCRIPT

Robbie: I'm Robbie the Rabbit. *(Cries.)* How do I feel? *(Let children respond.)* Yes, I feel SAD. I'm SAD BECAUSE Poppy the Pup will NOT play with me. I asked her to hop around the grass with me, and she said, "No. I do NOT like to hop around the grass."

Bring Poppy the Pup in on your other hand.

Robbie: Poppy! I want to hop around the grass. I like to hop around the grass.

Poppy: I don't. I do NOT like to hop around the grass.

Robbie: You don't want to play with me! I like to hop around the grass, and you do NOT want to. You don't like me. You won't play with me.

Poppy: I do NOT have to like hopping around the grass just BECAUSE you like to hop around the grass. I do like you. But DIFFERENT people like DIFFERENT things. Let's find the SAME thing that you like to do AND I like to do. Then we can play together.

Robbie: I like to look at flowers. Let's go look at flowers.

Poppy: You think that I like to look at flowers just BECAUSE you like to look at flowers. WHY don't you find out if I like to look at flowers?

Robbie: Do you like to look at flowers?

Poppy: No!

Robbie: Do you like to run?

Poppy: SOME of the time I do, and SOME of the time I do NOT. I ran all morning, and I do NOT want to run NOW. I do NOT like to run ALL of the time. MAYBE LATER I will want to run.

Robbie: I'm starting to feel FRUSTRATED. *(To the group)* Do you know WHY I'm feeling FRUSTRATED? *(Let children respond.)*

Yes, BECAUSE I'm trying DIFFERENT ways to get Poppy to play with me and she will NOT say yes. She says no or LATER to everything I think of. I'm going to ask her a DIFFERENT question.

(To Poppy) Poppy, what would *you* like to do?

Poppy: I'd like to sing.

Robbie: OK, I'd like that, too. I'm glad I asked you. I thought MAYBE you didn't want to play with me. We're friends, right?

Poppy: Right. *(To the group)* Would you like to sing with us?

Sing a song the children know, then ask what they learned from the puppet story. If needed, remind them that different people like different things and that it is important to find out what others like.

Robbie: *(To the group)* Listen carefully. These are hard questions. Who can think of something that:

You like AND your mother likes, too.

You like, but your mother does NOT like.

You like, but a 10-year-old boy would NOT like.

You like, but your grandmother does NOT like.

You do NOT like, but your father does like.

You do NOT like, but a 10-year-old girl MIGHT like.

Continue with similar questions as long as time and interest permit.

A Story

PURPOSE

To provide a review of ICPS concepts presented thus far

MATERIALS

Any storybook

TEACHER SCRIPT

Read any storybook to the group. If necessary, reread. At appropriate points, ask the following questions:

How did _____ feel when _____? *(Name a character and describe an event in the story.)*

How can you tell (he/she) felt that way? (*If needed:* Could you see the person with your eyes?)

WHY do you think (he/she) felt that way?

How did the person feel BEFORE (he/she) felt that way?

(If appropriate) Was it a good time or NOT a good time for the person to _____? *(Describe an action.)*

Remember to use ICPS word concepts whenever possible.

Sample Story

Read Will I Have a Friend? *by Miriam Cohen (MacMillan, 1967). If necessary, reread. At the point specified, ask these questions:*

After: "Sarah was telling Margaret a secret. Jim looked at them. Where was his friend?"

Did Sarah tell Margaret a secret OR did Sarah tell Susan a secret?

You know, Jimmy really wants a friend. Nobody is playing with him. How does Jimmy feel NOW?

WHY do you think he feels _____?

How did you feel the first day you came to school? Do you remember?

How do you feel NOW?

What happened to make you feel _____ NOW? (*If a negative feeling:* Can you think of something you can do to feel better/make a friend?)

My ICPS Book, Part II

PURPOSE

Like Lesson 30, to help children understand and express their feelings by drawing them

MATERIALS

Chalkboard or easel

Paper and crayons

Children's ICPS folders

TEACHER SCRIPT

Remember when you made drawings of things that made you feel HAPPY, SAD, ANGRY, or AFRAID?

This time, I want you to draw something you did today, something that happened to you, or anything you can think of that made you feel PROUD or FRUSTRATED.

After children have finished, ask them to tell you about their drawings. Write the feeling words on the chalkboard. If children can print, have them copy the appropriate feeling word from the board onto their drawings. If time permits, you or the children can write down what made them feel this way. Save the children's drawings in their individual ICPS folders.

Is That Fair?

PURPOSE

To help children think about their own and others' rights in decision making and to understand equal benefits when situations are equivalent

MATERIALS

A penny (or other small item) for each child

TEACHER SCRIPT

Today's ICPS lesson is about the word FAIR.

Give each child a penny.

I have a penny here for each of you, and I'm going to let each of you have one.

I have enough for each of you to have only one.

Is it FAIR for each of you to have one penny?

Yes, it is FAIR for each of you to have one BECAUSE I have only enough for each of you to have one.

If (Child 1) takes two pennies, then (Child 2) will NOT have any.

Ask the first child to take the second child's penny.

Now (Child 2) does NOT have a penny. Is that FAIR?

OK, (Child 1), how can you find out how (Child 2) feels NOW?
(*If needed:* Go ahead and ask.)

Repeat this sequence with a few other pairs of children so several will have the opportunity to ask another how he or she feels when something is taken away.

(*To Child 1*) What can you do so (Child 2) will feel HAPPY again?

Repeat with other children who took pennies. Be sure all the pennies are returned.

If two children want to look at the SAME storybook and one keeps it after he or she is finished with it, is that FAIR?

What is FAIR?

If two children want to play with the SAME toy at the SAME time, what is FAIR?

WHY is that FAIR?

What else is FAIR to do?

WHY is that FAIR?

If (Child 3) is the first in line today, is it FAIR for (him/her) to be first in line (tomorrow/next week)?

Is it FAIR for the SAME child to be first in line ALL of the time?

What is FAIR?

Throughout, continue to ask children why they think their ideas are or are not fair.

More About Fair, Version 1

PURPOSE

To illustrate that, in being FAIR, it is sometimes necessary to wait

MATERIALS

Enough chairs to build a pretend fire truck

TEACHER SCRIPT

> **NOTE**
> This lesson is good for kindergarten-age children; for first grade and older, try using Lesson 42.

Today we're going to talk about the word FAIR again.

Let's go on a pretend trip on this fire truck.

This fire truck is big enough to take only SOME of you.

It is NOT big enough to take ALL of you.

SOME of you can go NOW, and SOME of you can go LATER.

(Name half the children in the group) will go on our pretend trip NOW.

The rest of you *(name remaining children)* will have to wait and go LATER BECAUSE the fire truck is NOT big enough to take ALL of you at the SAME time.

The children over here *(point to the first half)* are going on the trip.

When will the rest of you get to go? *(If needed:* NOW or LATER?) Yes, LATER.

OK, wait for us here. We'll be back soon.

If you're going on the trip NOW, raise your hand.

If some children incorrectly identify themselves, help them get into the proper group.

OK, if you're going on the trip NOW, let's open the door and get inside the fire truck.

Go through the motion of opening the door and helping children get seated.

Let's all pretend that we're riding. *(Demonstrate by bouncing.)*

Can we make the sound of a siren?

I see lots of buildings! I see a flower!

We're riding through the streets!

What do you see?

Let each child name something.

Oh! There's the fire! Let's put it out. *(Pretend to spray water on the fire.)*

OK, the fire is out. Let's go back to school now.

Very good! Now we're back. We had a fun ride, didn't we?

Let's open the door and get out.

Now I'm going on another trip with SOME children.

We're going in the SAME fire truck, and I can take only SOME of you.

Who should go on the trip?

From raised hands, pick one child who did not go the first time and one who did.

Did (Child 1) go on the trip we took BEFORE? *(Name a child who did go on the first trip.)*

Did (Child 2) go on the trip we took BEFORE? *(Name a child who did not go.)*

Is it FAIR for (Child 2) to go NOW?

Yes, it is FAIR for (Child 2) to go now BECAUSE (he/she) did NOT go BEFORE. (He/she) did NOT go on the first trip.

Is it FAIR for (Child 1) to go NOW? Remember, (he/she) did go BEFORE, on the first trip.

WHY is it NOT FAIR for (Child 1) to go NOW?

Yes, it is NOT FAIR for (Child 1) to go NOW BECAUSE (he/she) went BEFORE, on the first trip.

We have to give ALL of the children a chance to go, but at DIFFERENT times.

Name the children in the group and ask whether or not each one went on the first trip. Then ask whether it would be fair for that child to go on the second trip, and why. Be sure to go on the pretend trip with the second group.

More About Fair, Version 2

PURPOSE

To illustrate that, in being FAIR, it is sometimes necessary to wait

MATERIALS

Enough chairs to build a pretend roller coaster

TEACHER SCRIPT

We're going to talk about the word FAIR again now.

Let's pretend we're at Disney World and we're going for a ride on a roller coaster.

Do you know what a roller coaster ride is?

Let me show you.

Demonstrate from a seated position by moving forward and backward, side to side, and by pretending to hold on to a bar in front of you with both hands.

The roller coaster has enough seats for only SOME of you. There are NOT enough seats for ALL of you at the SAME time.

SOME of you can go on the ride NOW, and SOME of you can go on the ride LATER.

Have half of the class come to the front of the room. Seat these children side by side in pairs in the pretend roller coaster.

These children are going on the roller coaster ride NOW.

When will the rest of you get to go? NOW or LATER?

Yes, LATER.

OK, wait for us here. We'll be back soon.

OK, fasten your seat belts: "Click!" Ready?

OK, the roller coaster is moving. Hold on.

We are climbing up the hill—higher, higher, higher, higher.

You're as high as the trees. Get ready. Hold on tight.

We're going down the hill.

Woooooooooooo!

Feel the wind blow through your hair.

Feel the excitement in your body.

Smell the popcorn in the air.

Hear the people laughing.

OK, we're climbing again. Hold on.

And ahhhh, down we goooooo!

Put your arms up. Wooooooo!

And now the ride is over.

Oh, we had a fun ride, didn't we?

Let's unfasten our seat belts *(pretend to do so)* and get out of the roller coaster.

Help children get out.

Now I'm going on another trip with SOME children.

We're going on the SAME roller coaster ride, and I can take only SOME of you.

Who should go on the trip this time?

Did (Child 1) go on the first trip, the trip we took BEFORE? *(Name a child who did not go.)*

Is it FAIR for (Child 1) to go NOW?

WHY is it FAIR for (him/her) to go NOW?

Yes, it is FAIR for (Child 1) to go NOW BECAUSE (he/she) did NOT go BEFORE, on the first trip.

Did (Child 2) go on the first trip, the trip we took BEFORE? *(Name a child who did go.)*

Is it FAIR for (Child 2) to go NOW? Remember, (he/she) did go BEFORE, on the first trip.

WHY is it NOT FAIR for (Child 2) to go NOW?

Yes, it is NOT FAIR for (Child 2) to go NOW BECAUSE (he/she) went on the first trip.

We have to give ALL the children a chance to go, but at DIFFERENT times.

Take the second group of children on the pretend roller coaster ride.

Fair or Not Fair?

When a child is exhibiting dominating behaviors:

Is it FAIR for you to have ALL the turns and for others NOT to have any?

How do people feel when they want a chance to say something and you keep shouting out?

Choose a child who has NOT had a turn to talk.

When a child refuses to take turns or share:

Is it FAIR for you to have ALL the turns and for _____ NOT to have any?

How MIGHT _____ feel if you do NOT let him play with that?

You played with that BEFORE. _____ did NOT have a turn with it.

Is it FAIR for you to play NOW?

Can you think of something DIFFERENT to do NOW?

Did _____ finish (his/her) turn with that?

Is it FAIR for you to take that BEFORE (he/she) has finished a turn?

Is it FAIR for you to have your turn BEFORE or AFTER (he/she) has finished a turn?

Fair or Not Fair?

NEWS AND EVENTS OF THE DAY

Did you do anything today that was NOT FAIR?

What could you have done to be FAIR?

Did anyone do anything to you today that was NOT FAIR?

What could (he/she) have done to be FAIR?

READING AND STORY COMPREHENSION

(About an appropriate story) Is what happened in this story FAIR or NOT FAIR?

WHY is that (FAIR/NOT FAIR)? *(If not fair:* What could have happened that would be FAIR?)

MATH

(Child 1) turns a rope 8 times, and (Child 2) turns it 4 times.

Who turned the rope more times, (Child 1) or (Child 2)?

If (Child 3) jumps the rope 10 times and (Child 4) jumps 10 times, what is true?

- (Child 3) had more jumps than (Child 4). Yes or no?
- (Child 4) had more jumps than (Child 3). Yes or no?
- (Child 3) AND (Child 4) had the SAME number of jumps. Yes or no?

If the rope belongs to the school, what is FAIR?

- For (Child 3) to have more jumps than (Child 4). Yes or no?
- For (Child 4) to have more jumps than (Child 3). Yes or no?
- For (Child 3) AND (Child 4) to have the SAME number of jumps. Yes or no?

If a child says it is fair for someone to have more jumps, do not correct. Ask the child why he or she thinks that.

Three kids on Team A hit 1 home run each.

One kid on Team B hit 3 home runs.

What is true?

- Team A had more home runs than Team B.
- Team B had more home runs than Team A.
- Team A AND Team B had the SAME number of home runs.

Impatient

PURPOSE

To help children understand the feeling of impatience in order to guide behavior in problem solving

MATERIALS

Chalkboard or easel

TEACHER SCRIPT

Today we have a new ICPS feeling word. The word is IMPATIENT.

When you want something NOW and have to wait until LATER, you MIGHT feel IMPATIENT.

If you want some candy NOW and you have to wait until LATER, MAYBE until after dinner, you MIGHT feel IMPATIENT BECAUSE you want it NOW.

When Poppy wanted Dilly to play with her and Dilly was busy talking to a friend, Poppy felt FRUSTRATED, but soon she became IMPATIENT. WHY?

BECAUSE she had to wait and wait and wait.

Have you ever had to wait and wait for something, and you felt IMPATIENT?

Tell us about it.

How did that make you feel?

Let's make up a story using the word IMPATIENT.

If there is a Luisa or Crystal in your class, you will want to change the names in the following example.

Crystal is 4 years old.

Luisa is 6 years old. She is Crystal's sister.

Crystal is looking at a storybook.

Luisa wants the book NOW. She can NOT wait until LATER.

How is Luisa feeling? (*If needed:* What's our big new feeling word?)

Yes, Luisa is feeling IMPATIENT. She wants the book NOW. So guess what she does.

Oh, she grabs the book out of her sister's hands.

How do you think her sister, Crystal, feels when Luisa does that?

What happens next in this story? Make it up.

Write the story on the chalkboard as it unfolds. If children do not spontaneously attempt to solve the problem, ask, "How do you think Luisa and Crystal can solve this problem?" After children have suggested a solution, test their story comprehension by asking the following questions:

Is Crystal Luisa's sister OR is she her friend?

Was Crystal OR Luisa reading the storybook?

When Luisa wanted the storybook NOW and could NOT wait until LATER, how was she feeling?

When Luisa felt IMPATIENT, what did she do next? (*If needed:* What did she do to get the storybook?)

How did that make Crystal feel?

Did Crystal feel ANGRY BEFORE or AFTER Luisa snatched her book?

What did you say happened next in the story?

Did that happen BEFORE or AFTER Crystal and Luisa solved the problem?

How did they solve the problem?

HINT

Call on generally nonresponsive children to answer easy comprehension questions. If needed, repeat key words. For example, you might add to the first comprehension question the key words "sister OR friend?" Giving a choice requires the child to say only one word.

Let's Make Up a Story, Part III

PURPOSE

To help children understand sequencing, for later comprehension of steps in problem solving

MATERIALS

Chalkboard or easel

TEACHER SCRIPT

Use names different from those of children in the class.

Robin, Monique, and Sandra were laughing and jumping rope together.

They were having a good time.

They felt very _____. (*If needed:* HAPPY or SAD?)

And Monique learned a new trick and did it very well.

She felt _____.

Yes, she felt PROUD of herself.

Well, this rope was very old.

When Robin started jumping again, the old rope broke in half.

The girls wanted to jump more, but they could NOT BECAUSE the rope was broken.

Now they felt _____. (*If needed:* HAPPY or FRUSTRATED?)

Well, Tonya, Kim, and Leah came along with their rope, and they started jumping.

Robin and Sandra went home, but Monique asked if she could have a turn.

Tonya said, "Yes, but you have to wait your turn."

So Monique waited, but Tonya and Kim and Leah kept on jumping and jumping and jumping.

Monique wanted to jump NOW. She started to feel _____.
(*If needed:* HAPPY or IMPATIENT?)

Yes, IMPATIENT. She asked them . . .

What happens next in the story? You make it up.

Write the story on the chalkboard as it unfolds. Encourage several children to add to the story. When finished, test the children's story comprehension by asking the following questions:

> What happened to the rope that made Robin, Monique, and Sandra feel FRUSTRATED?
>
> How did Monique feel when Tonya and Kim and Leah kept jumping and jumping with their rope?
>
> WHY did Monique feel IMPATIENT?
>
> Then what happened in the story?

Develop more questions based on the children's additions to the story.

What Can I Do While I Wait?

PURPOSE

To help children cope with frustration when their needs cannot be satisfied immediately

MATERIALS

None

TEACHER SCRIPT

Today we're going to think about what you can do while you wait. Doing things while you wait can help you feel good instead of FRUSTRATED and IMPATIENT.

I'm going to tell you some things that kids MIGHT want to have or do, but they have to wait.

Use names different from those of children in the class.

Example 1

Rafael and Paul are playing after school.

Rafael wants to play with Paul's wagon, but Paul has just started playing with it.

Paul says, "You can have it when I'm finished."

What can Rafael do while he waits?

Tell me three things you could do if you had to wait like this.

Example 2

Sarah wants her teacher to help her with her puzzle, but her teacher is busy helping someone else.

Is it a good time or NOT a good time for Sarah to ask for help?

What can Sarah do while she waits?

Tell me three things you could do if you had to wait like this.

Example 3

Thomas wants to tell his mother something, but his mother is busy talking on the phone.

Is this a good time or NOT a good time for Thomas to try to talk to his mother?

What can Thomas do while he waits?

Tell me three things you could do if you had to wait like this.

Now you think of a time when you had to wait for something.

What happened?

What could you have done while you waited?

What did we learn from this? (*If needed:* If you do something else while you wait, it doesn't seem like such a long time to get help, talk to your mother, and so on.)

ICPS Word: Impatient

When a child refuses to take turns or share:

> If you will NOT take turns or share, and if someone has to wait and wait and wait for a turn, is that FAIR?
>
> How MIGHT the person feel?
>
> *If needed:* At first, FRUSTRATED, and then _____. What's our big new word?
>
> *If still needed:* IMPATIENT or AFRAID?

When a class is noisy:

> If you keep talking while I'm trying to teach you, and I have to wait and wait and wait, how do you think I'm feeling?
>
> *If needed:* At first, FRUSTRATED, BECAUSE I cannot teach.
>
> Then when I have to wait and wait, I feel _____. (HAPPY or IMPATIENT?)

When a child can't wait:

> Sometimes you feel IMPATIENT when someone else really does take too long to do something.
>
> For instance, you MIGHT feel IMPATIENT when someone takes too long a turn with a toy or too long a drink at the water fountain.
>
> But when you want something BEFORE it's your turn, and you can NOT wait, you're also being IMPATIENT.
>
> I know it can be hard to wait, but sometimes it is FAIR to wait.
>
> What can you do NOW while you wait for your turn?

Worried-Relieved

PURPOSE

To help children become aware of these feelings in themselves and others

MATERIALS

None

TEACHER SCRIPT

Use names different from those of children in the class.

Today's ICPS game is about two new words, WORRIED and RELIEVED.

First, the word WORRIED: Does anyone know what that means?

People can WORRY that bad things or SAD things MIGHT happen.

Peter wants to pass his math test—you know, do really well— but he thinks he MIGHT NOT.

He is WORRIED about that.

Carline loves to go to the zoo, and she is going on Saturday.

She is WORRIED that it MIGHT rain BECAUSE if it rains she can NOT go to the zoo.

What WORRIES you?

People can also WORRY about other people.

James's mother is WORRIED BECAUSE James is not home yet.

He should have been home by now, and he is NOT.

Where is he? She is WORRIED.

Sherry is high up in a tree.

Her friend is WORRIED that she MIGHT fall.

Have you ever worried about someone else?

Have you ever done anything that made your mother or father feel WORRIED?

Now let's talk about the word RELIEVED.

When someone is WORRIED about something and it turns out OK, that person feels RELIEVED.

Peter was WORRIED that he would NOT pass his math test.

He did very well. He felt RELIEVED.

How did Peter feel BEFORE he took his math test?

How did he feel AFTER he passed it and did very well?

Carline was WORRIED that it MIGHT rain and she could NOT go to the zoo.

It was sunny, and she got to go to the zoo.

When she woke up and looked out the window and saw the sun, she felt RELIEVED.

People can also feel RELIEVED about other people.

James's mother was WORRIED when James was NOT home.

When he came home, she felt RELIEVED.

When Sherry was high up in the tree, her friend felt WORRIED that she MIGHT fall.

When Sherry got down and was OK, her friend felt RELIEVED.

Repeat what children said made them feel worried, then ask how the situation turned out and how they felt before and after.

Find a Feelings Match

PURPOSE

To help children pay careful attention

MATERIALS

Illustrations 14–21, copied and mounted on posterboard

TEACHER SCRIPT

NOTE

Begin with the number of illustrations you think your class can handle and increase as needed. For six children, make two copies of three different illustrations and give each child one. For eight children, make two copies of four different illustrations, and so forth. Children with illustrations are the "panel." The rest of the group are the "players."

Have panel members come to the front and stand with the illustrations against their chests, with the blank sides showing.

I want (Player 1) to name someone holding a picture.

(To the panel member holding the illustration) Turn your picture around so we can ALL see it.

(To all players) Look at this picture carefully and remember who has it. The idea of this game is to find another picture that is the SAME. When you do, you will have a match.

(To Player 1) Now name another child holding a picture.

(To the panel member holding the illustration) Turn your picture around so we can ALL see it.

(To all players) Is this the SAME picture OR a DIFFERENT picture?

If different: OK, both of you turn your cards around so we can NOT see the pictures. (Player 2), now you call the name of a child holding a card.

If the same: Oh, you made a match.

(To all players) How does the child in this picture feel?

WHY do you think (he/she) MIGHT be feeling that way?

What makes you feel that way?

Encourage the use of the word PROUD if Illustrations 16 or 17 are the ones matched. If a child says "happy," say, "HAPPY and _____?"

Next place all the illustrations faceup so children can see them.

Find two children who feel a DIFFERENT way about the SAME thing.

When children identify Illustration 21:

How do you think these two girls feel?

WHY MIGHT this girl *(point)* feel ANGRY about listening to music?

Any other reason? Another BECAUSE?

WHY MIGHT this other girl *(point)* feel HAPPY about the same music?

Any other reason? Another BECAUSE?

ILLUSTRATION 14 Lesson 47

ILLUSTRATION 15 Lesson 47

ILLUSTRATION 16   Lesson 47

ILLUSTRATION 17 Lesson 47

ILLUSTRATION 18   Lesson 47

ILLUSTRATION 19 Lesson 47

ILLUSTRATION 20   Lesson 47

ILLUSTRATION 21   Lesson 47

All ICPS Feeling Words

NEWS AND EVENTS OF THE DAY

Did anything happen to anybody (*Or:* Was anything in the news) today that made you feel HAPPY, SAD, ANGRY, AFRAID, PROUD, FRUSTRATED, IMPATIENT, WORRIED, or RELIEVED?

Did you do anything today to make someone else feel any of these ways?

READING AND STORY COMPREHENSION

At an appropriate time in a story you read, ask how a character felt. Encourage the use of "our big new feeling words."

MATH

Draw two clocks, one at 4:00 and the other at 6:00.

Your mother said to come home at 4:00 and you came home at 6:00:

- Is 6:00 BEFORE or AFTER 4:00?
- How MIGHT your mother feel if you are NOT home when you are supposed to be and she does NOT know where you are? (*If needed:* WORRIED or HAPPY?)
- Is 6:00 a good time or NOT a good time to come home if you should be home at 4:00?

SOCIAL STUDIES

If the boat that brought the pilgrims to America stopped and did not move for a long time, how MIGHT the people feel?

How would they feel AFTER the boat moved again?

How would George Washington feel if his soldiers did not show up for the battle on time?

How MIGHT George Washington have felt BEFORE he won the battle?

And AFTER he won?

PROBLEM-SOLVING SKILLS

ALTERNATIVE SOLUTIONS

The lessons in this section help children learn that there is more than one way to solve a problem. In particular, they stimulate children to think of as many different solutions as possible to everyday interpersonal problems and encourage a *process* of thinking: "There's more than one way"; "I don't have to give up too soon."

PROCEDURE

As used in the lessons, the general procedure for eliciting alternative solutions is as follows:

1. State the problem or have the child state the problem.

2. Say that the idea is to think of lots of DIFFERENT ways to solve this problem.

3. Write all of the children's ideas on chalkboard or easel. (Even though some children may not be able to read, they like your writing what they say.)

4. Ask for the first solution. If the solution is relevant, repeat it and identify it as *one* way to solve the problem. Remind children that the object is to think of lots of DIFFERENT ways to solve the problem.

5. Ask for another solution, and so forth.

6. When ideas run out, probe for further solutions by asking, "What can _____ say to *(repeat problem)*?" and "What can _____ do to *(repeat problem)*?"

ENUMERATIONS

Children often give variations of the same solution. For example:

- *Giving something:* Give him candy, give him gum, give him a cookie.
- *Hurting someone:* Hit him, kick him, bite him.
- *Telling someone:* Tell his mother, father, sister.

An effective way of dealing with enumerations is to say, for example, "Giving candy and giving gum are kind of the SAME BECAUSE they are both giving something. Can you think of something DIFFERENT from giving

225

something?" After a while, you can ask children to identify for themselves how enumerations show the same kinds of ideas.

Avoid saying, "That's good" or "That's a good idea" in response to a given solution. If you focus on the *content* of what children say, they will think you like a particular idea and you will likely get more enumerations. If you do say *good*, focus on the *process* by saying, "Good, that's a DIFFERENT idea."

UNCLEAR OR
APPARENTLY IRRELEVANT RESPONSES

If a child gives an unclear or apparently irrelevant response, it is important to ask, "WHY do you think that will solve this problem?" or to say, "Tell us a little more about that." Often a response that is unclear or seems irrelevant is actually quite logical.

Take, for instance, the problem of a boy's wanting an extra piece of cake at school. The solution "He'll say he'll get fat" may appear to be a consequence of eating the cake (a concept to come later). You might be tempted to assume that the response is therefore irrelevant to the present lesson. However, if you ask, "How would that help the boy get the cake?" the child might say, "Because he's too skinny, and his mom wants him to eat more." The new information shows that the response "He'll say he'll get fat" is indeed a solution—a way to help the boy get the extra cake. If on clarification a response actually does turn out to be a consequence instead of a solution, acknowledge the response and elicit a solution by asking, "What can the boy do or say to solve the problem?"

"He will cry" is another response requiring clarification. If in the case of the boy who wants the extra cake the response is simply a *reaction* to the problem's existence, it is irrelevant because it is not a solution to the problem. If, on the other hand, the response is intended to gain sympathy, it is a *cognitive cry*—and therefore a solution. If a child gives this response, always ask him or her to tell you more.

What Else Can He Do? Part I

PURPOSE

To encourage children to think of as many solutions to a problem
as they can

MATERIALS

Illustration 22

Chalkboard or easel

TEACHER SCRIPT

Show children Illustration 22.

The problem in this picture is that this boy *(point)* wants his mother
to buy him this box of cookies.

What does the boy want his mother to do?

Right, buy him the box of cookies.

Now we're going to play the What Else Can He Do Game.

We want to think of lots of ways, lots of DIFFERENT solutions
to this problem.

I'm going to write ALL your ideas to solve the problem on the
chalkboard.

Who's got way number one? *(Show one finger.)*

*Write each response as given to form a numbered list. Even though some
children won't be able to read, writing their ideas on the board is an effective
motivating technique.*

RESPONSE: He could ask her. *(Write this on the board, as the
example shows.)*

1. He could ask her.

If response is relevant: That's *one* way. Now the idea of this game is to think of lots of DIFFERENT ways to solve the problem.

If response is not relevant: How would that help solve the problem?

OK, he could ask her. That's *one* way.

Now the idea of this game is to think of lots of DIFFERENT ways this boy can get his mother to buy him the cookies.

Who's got way number two? Let's fill up the whole board.

RESPONSE: He could say, "I'll share them with my sister." *(Add to the list.)*

1. He could ask her.
2. He could say, "I'll share them with my sister."

OK, he could ask her, or he could say he'll share them with his sister. Now we have two ways.

I bet you can think of lots of DIFFERENT ways.

Who can think of way three?

RESPONSE: He could let his brother have some. *(Enumeration— write under the like response, not as a separate solution.)*

1. He could ask her.
2. He could say, "I'll share them with my sister."
   He could let his brother have some.

Oh, sharing with his sister and letting his brother have some are kind of the SAME BECAUSE _____. *(If needed:* They are both examples of sharing.)

Can you think of something DIFFERENT from sharing?

RESPONSE: He could cry. *(Unclear response—clarify.)*

Tell me more about that.

228

RESPONSE: So his mom will feel sorry for him. *(Add to the list.)*

1. He could ask her.
2. He could say, "I'll share them with my sister."
   He could let his brother have some.
3. He could cry so his mom will feel sorry for him.

If the child says the boy would cry because he can't get the box of cookies, the response is irrelevant because it is a reaction to frustration, not a way to solve the problem. Say, "He MIGHT cry, but what can he do or say so his mom will buy the cookies?" In this case, the response is a way to get the mom to give in and therefore a relevant solution.

OK, he could cry so his mom will feel sorry for him and buy the cookies. That's way three.

Who has a DIFFERENT way?

RESPONSE: He could say, "I'll only eat a few." *(Add to the list.)*

RESPONSE: He could tell her he'll wait till after dinner. *(Add to the list.)*

RESPONSE: He could say, "They'll help me grow." *(Add to the list.)*

OK, we have six ways this boy can try to get his mom to buy him this box of cookies.

Remember to summarize all the solutions presented. When finished, the board will look like the example provided.

1. He could ask her.
2. He could say, "I'll share them with my sister."
   He could let his brother have some.
3. He could cry so his mom will feel sorry for him.
4. He could say, "I'll only eat a few."
5. He could tell her he'll wait till after dinner.
6. He could say, "They'll help me grow."

HINT

Classify all enumerations as only one solution. For example, about the possible responses "He'll eat them later" and "He'll eat them after dinner," you might say, "That's *one* way. Eating them later and after dinner are both waiting. Now can you think of something DIFFERENT from waiting?" Another common enumeration involves taking the cookies surreptitiously—for example, "Put them under the food in the cart" and "Hide them under his shirt." Ask, "Can you think of something DIFFERENT from hiding them?"

Avoid saying "That's a good idea." If you say *good,* say, "Good, that's a DIFFERENT idea." If children think you like a given idea, you'll only get more enumerations.

ILLUSTRATION 22   Lesson 48

What Else Can He Do? Part II

PURPOSE

To give children additional practice in thinking of as many solutions to a problem as they can

MATERIALS

Illustration 23

Chalkboard or easel

TEACHER SCRIPT

Show children Illustration 23.

> This boy *(point)* broke his sister's doll, and she's feeling _____.
> (*If needed:* ANGRY or SAD?)
>
> What did this boy do?
>
> Right, he broke his sister's doll.
>
> Now we're going to play the What Else Can He Do Game again. Remember, we want to think of lots of DIFFERENT ways to solve this problem.

Use the techniques illustrated in Lesson 48 to elicit alternative solutions from children.

HINT

Once again, watch for enumerations. Common ones relating to this problem will concern ways to fix the doll: "Glue it," "Tape it," "Paste it," and so forth. Also common are ways of apologizing: "I'm sorry," "I won't do it again," "Excuse me," and the like.

ILLUSTRATION 23 Lesson 49

What's That Problem? Part I

PURPOSE

To illustrate that one cannot assume what a problem is

MATERIALS

Illustration 24

Feeling face stickers, duplicated from Lesson 30 (one each of HAPPY, SAD, ANGRY, and AFRAID for each child)

TEACHER SCRIPT

> **NOTE**
> Children may draw the feeling faces instead of using the feeling stickers.

Give each child a copy of Illustration 24.

Look at this picture carefully. Look at each child in the picture.

Pick someone you think has a problem.

Choose a feeling sticker and put it on the face of the child you think has the problem.

Put on the *one* feeling sticker that you think shows how the child feels.

When children are finished:

(Child 1), who do you think has the problem in this picture?

What feeling sticker did you put on (his/her) face?

(Child 2), who do you think has the problem in this picture?

What feeling sticker did you put on (his/her) face?

Did (Child 1) and (Child 2) pick the SAME child OR a DIFFERENT child?

Did they think these children had the SAME feeling OR a DIFFERENT feeling?

Repeat with as many children as time and interest permit.

Did ALL of you see the SAME problem?

Did SOME of you see a DIFFERENT problem?

What did we learn from this?

If needed: When we see kids in this room doing things that make us think they have a problem, do we know what the problem is just by seeing with our eyes? How can we find out what the problem is?

If still needed: We can ask.

ILLUSTRATION 24   Lesson 50

Solve the Problem

PURPOSE

To illustrate that there is more than one way to solve a problem

MATERIALS

Illustration 24 (children's copies from Lesson 50)

Chalkboard or easel

TEACHER SCRIPT

Choose a child to come to the front with his or her illustration from Lesson 50. Ask the child to state the problem as he or she sees it. If the problem is not interpersonal (for example, "The boy's shoelace is broken") prompt the child to think of a problem between people.

> *(To the child)* What can the child do to solve this problem?
> *(Let child respond.)*
>
> That's *one* way.
>
> Remember, the idea of this game is to think of lots of DIFFERENT ways to solve this problem.
>
> *(To the group)* Who's got way number two? Let's fill up the whole chalkboard.

Continue to generate alternative solutions, writing each one on the board. When ideas run out, call on a child who has chosen a different problem and repeat the process. If time permits, let each child choose a second feeling face sticker to place on another child in the picture.

HINT

If a child is unable to name an interpersonal problem, call on someone else. Remember to classify or let children classify enumerations. For example:

- Giving something (candy, gum, cookies)
- Telling someone (mother, father, sister)
- Hurting someone (hitting, kicking, biting)

My ICPS Book, Part III

PURPOSE

To show children how to express interpersonal problems by drawing them

MATERIALS

Paper and crayons

Children's ICPS folders

TEACHER SCRIPT

Today I want you to draw a problem.

This could be something that really happened, or you could just make it up.

It could be something between two kids, you and your mom, or anybody.

Show how each person in your picture is feeling.

As children draw, circulate and write the problem for as many children as time allows (see the sample drawing provided). Later, on the same or a different day, invite children to share their pictures.

(*To a child*) _____, come up and show us your picture.

Tell us the problem.

Now tell us a way to solve this problem.

That's *one* way. We always want to think of lots of ways.

Who can think of a DIFFERENT way?

Elicit alternative solutions in the usual way. Let children save their pictures in their ICPS folders. If desired, place some on the wall for display.

SAMPLE DRAWING: INTERPERSONAL PROBLEM

The children are fighting over the stick.

Finding Solutions

REASONS AND SOLUTIONS

When a child pushes in line (or engages in similar behavior):

(To the group) WHY do people push in line?

WHY else? Can you give me another BECAUSE?

Elicit as many reasons as possible.

(To the child who pushed) What was your reason?

What else could you do so _____? *(Repeat child's reason.)*

MINI-DIALOGUES

In each of these examples, the teacher asks, "What happened?" (getting the child's perspective of the problem), "How do you feel?" (guiding the child to think about feelings), and "What can you say or do?" (guiding the child to think of alternative solutions).

Situation 1: Marianne is restricted from free play.

Teacher: What's the matter? WHY aren't you playing?

Marianne: I don't know.

Teacher: You don't know? Something must have happened.

Marianne: Mr. James took away my playtime.

Teacher: WHY?

Marianne: BECAUSE Samuel kept messing with me during rest time.

Teacher: So Mr. James took away your playtime BECAUSE you and Samuel were not resting? How do you think Mr. James felt when you were not resting?

Marianne: ANGRY.

Teacher: ANGRY, huh? Is that WHY he took away your playtime?

Marianne: Yes.

Teacher: How do you feel about losing your playtime?

Marianne: SAD.

Teacher: What is something you can do or say the next time someone messes with you so no one feels SAD or ANGRY?

Marianne:	I could tell the teacher.
Teacher:	OK, that's *one* idea. Can you think of something else that MIGHT work?
Marianne:	I could tell him to stop.
Teacher:	That's another idea. Great, you thought of two ideas. MAYBE you could try those next time.

Situation 2: Alberto and Thomas are pushing and fighting in the classroom, scrambling to sit in a single seat.

Teacher:	What's going on? What's the matter? That will help me understand the problem better.
Alberto:	He's sitting in my seat.
Thomas:	Hey, he's sitting in *my* seat.
Teacher:	Do you two see this the SAME way or a DIFFERENT way?
Thomas:	DIFFERENT.
Teacher:	That means we have a problem. How do you feel?
Alberto:	ANGRY!
Teacher:	How do you feel, Thomas?
Thomas:	SAD.
Teacher:	So you feel ANGRY, and you feel SAD. Is there something either of you can do to make it better?
Thomas:	Sit apart.
Teacher:	That's *one* way. How can you find out if that is OK with Alberto?
Thomas:	*(To Alberto)* Is that OK?
Alberto:	I want to be friends.
Teacher:	You want to be friends. Do you want that, Thomas?
Thomas:	*(Thinks and nods.)* Yes.
Teacher:	OK, what can you do to be friends?
Alberto:	NOT fight.
Teacher:	What can you two do if you do NOT fight?
Alberto:	*(Shakes hands with Thomas and walks off arm in arm with him.)*

Situation 3: Susan and Troy fight continually at the lunch table.

Teacher:	What's going on over there? What's the matter?
Susan:	He hit me.
Troy:	She keeps messing with me.
Teacher:	Do you see this the SAME way or a DIFFERENT way?
Susan:	A DIFFERENT way.
Teacher:	That means we have a problem. How do you feel, Susan?
Susan:	Mad.
Teacher:	How do you feel, Troy?
Troy:	Mad.
Teacher:	So you both feel mad. Is there something you can do or say so you both don't feel mad?
Susan:	My mom says to hit back if a kid hits me.
Teacher:	That's *one* way, but it's not the only way. Can you think of another way?
Susan:	No.
Teacher:	Let's get the class to help. *(To the group)* Can anyone think of a way these children can solve their problem?
Lindsay:	They could talk it out.
Teacher:	That's *one* way. Can you think of another way?
Doyle:	They could say sorry.
Teacher:	OK, that's another way. Can you think of a third way, way number three?
Marcus:	They could be friends.
Teacher:	We thought of three ways to solve this problem. Susan and Troy, would you like to choose a way to make things better?
Troy:	We could talk it out.
Teacher:	Go ahead and try that.

Note that the teacher does not say, "We don't hit in school" when Susan offers the idea as a solution. If a parent has told a child that this is an acceptable response, the contradiction would only be confusing. Instead, the teacher helps the children identify nonaggressive solutions. This teacher also asks other children to help when the ones involved in the problem cannot think of any solutions. The message will have more impact if children think on their own or get help from their peers than if the teacher tells them what to do.

A Story

PURPOSE

To encourage story comprehension and further understanding of feelings

MATERIALS

Any storybook

TEACHER SCRIPT

Read any storybook to the class. If necessary, reread. At appropriate points, ask the following questions:

How MIGHT _____ feel when _____? *(Name a character and describe an event in the story.)*

What else can _____ do so that will NOT happen?

(When appropriate) How does _____ feel?

WHY does _____ feel that way?

Sample Story

Read The Circus Baby, *by Maud and Miska Petersham (MacMillan, 1950). If necessary, reread. At the following specified points, ask these questions:*

After: ''Mother elephant decided that her baby must learn to eat just as the circus people did.''

Elephants eat with their trunks. *(Imitate this action.)*

People eat with their _____?

Do elephants and people eat the SAME way?

No, they eat _____ ways. *(If needed: SAME or DIFFERENT?)*

After: "The bowl tipped and clattered off the table. Then Mr. Clown's stool gave a loud creak and split into many pieces."

How will Mr. and Mrs. Clown feel when they see this?

What could you do if you spilled everything on the floor?

What else could you do?

Let's see what happens in *this* story.

Continue with the story.

Introduction to Role-Playing

PURPOSE

To show children how to role-play an action, preliminary to later role-playing of problem situations

MATERIALS

None

TEACHER SCRIPT

Today we're going to play pretend.

We are going to do things that you can see with your eyes but can NOT hear with your ears. When we do this, we do NOT talk.

Make motion of brushing teeth.

What do you think I am doing?

Very good, I am pretending to brush my teeth.

Let's see ALL of you pretend to brush your teeth, too.

Very good.

Make motion of tying your shoe.

Now what am I doing?

Very good. I am pretending to tie my shoe.

OK, now I need a leader.

Choose a child to come up front.

I am going to whisper an idea in the leader's ear, and the leader is going to pretend to do it.

Watch the leader very carefully. You guess what (he/she) is doing.

Whisper one of the following actions in the leader's ear:

- Washing face
- Playing hopscotch
- Reading a book
- Eating pizza
- Getting dressed
- Playing basketball
- Jumping rope
- Blowing nose
- Singing
- Playing ball
- Sweeping the floor
- Dancing

Repeat with new leaders as time and interest permit. Add any other actions you wish to the list, or let the leader think of a "guessable" idea. If necessary, remind the leader not to talk.

Guess the Problem

PURPOSE

To stress the need to get information and understand motivation before making assumptions and to reinforce the idea that there is more than one way

MATERIALS

None

TEACHER SCRIPT

Today we're going to start with a guessing game.

To play this game, some of you are going to pretend a problem, act it out, and NOT talk—just like before, when we pretended to brush our teeth.

Bring four children to the front. Whisper the following role-play situation for them to act out:

(To two children) You two pretend to turn a jump rope.

(To the third) You pretend to jump.

(To the fourth) You pretend to push _____ while (he/she) is jumping.

(After the role-play, to the class) Can you guess what the problem is?

If the first guess is incorrect:

You can NOT always tell what the problem is right away.

You have to find out.

After children guess:

Is pushing like that a good idea?

WHY do you think someone would do that? BECAUSE _____.

WHY else?

How MIGHT the child who is jumping feel?

Who can think of a DIFFERENT way to _____?
(Repeat reason given.)

Invite the child who thinks of a different way to role-play the idea. After the role-play, bring four new children to the front. Whisper the following situation for them to act out:

> *(To three children)* You all stand in line.
>
> *(To the fourth)* You get ahead of everyone else in line.
>
> *(After the role-play, to the class)* Can you guess what the problem is?

After children guess:

> Is getting ahead in line like that a good idea?
>
> WHY would someone do that? BECAUSE_____.
>
> WHY else?
>
> How MIGHT the others in line feel about that?
>
> Who can think of a DIFFERENT way to _____?
> *(Repeat reason given.)*

Encourage the child who thinks of a different way to role-play the idea. After the role-play, bring four more children to the front. Whisper the following situation for them to act out:

> *(To three children)* You all pretend to be eating food.
>
> *(To the fourth)* You pretend to throw food.
>
> *(After the role-play, to the class)* Can you guess what the problem is?

After children guess:

> Is throwing food like that a good idea?
>
> WHY would someone do that? BECAUSE_____.
>
> WHY else?
>
> How MIGHT the others feel about that?
>
> Who can think of a DIFFERENT way to _____?
> *(Repeat reason given.)*

Have the child who thinks of a different way role-play the idea. After the role-play, bring four new children to the front. Whisper the following situation for them to act out:

> *(To three children)* You all talk to one another.
>
> *(To one of the three)* You shake your head no at (the fourth child).
>
> *(To the fourth)* You stand a little away from the other three and look as though you want to play with them.
>
> This one is a little harder. Who can guess what this problem is?

After children guess:

WHY MIGHT these three children NOT want to play with _____?

WHY else? Just make up reasons.

What can _____ do or say to get to play with the others?

That's *one* thing. Who can think of a DIFFERENT way?

Invite the child who thinks of a different way to role-play the idea.

HINT

Elicit alternative solutions in the usual way and encourage children to classify enumerations as they arise. Try using these kinds of questions when real situations come up in the classroom.

Puppet Story: Preferences and Solutions

PURPOSE

To help children become aware that it often helps to find out others' preferences in order to solve a problem

MATERIALS

Any two hand puppets (for example, Dilly the Duck and Poppy the Pup)

Chalkboard or easel

TEACHER SCRIPT

Dilly: Poppy, I know you're mad at me BECAUSE I wouldn't play with you yesterday, but would you come and play with me NOW?

Poppy: No!

Dilly: *(To the group)* Uh-oh. I have to think of a way to get Poppy to play with me again. She's very ANGRY with me. Can you help me think of a way?

Child: *(Offers a possible solution.)*

Dilly: *(To Poppy)* Will you play with me if I do that?

Poppy: No. I'm still very ANGRY.

Dilly: *(To the group)* Oh, you'll have to think of something DIFFERENT. Poppy is still ANGRY.

Elicit alternative solutions and write each one on the chalkboard. After children run out of ideas, ask them what Dilly has to find out about Poppy before he picks one of these solutions. If needed, remind them that they can ask "Do you like?"

More Role-Plays With Puppets

PURPOSE

To encourage generation of more alternative solutions and help children see that they do not need to give up too soon

MATERIALS

Any two hand puppets (for example, Dilly the Duck and Poppy the Pup)

Chalkboard or easel

TEACHER SCRIPT

Today we're going to play a guessing game again.

Just as we did before, we're going to pretend a problem— act it out—and NOT talk.

Bring two children to the front and let each of them choose a puppet. Whisper to both that Dilly should pretend to grab a toy from Poppy.

Can you guess what the problem is?

(After the problem is identified) Is grabbing a toy a good idea?

WHY MIGHT someone do this?

How MIGHT Poppy feel when Dilly grabbed her toy?

Who can think of a DIFFERENT way to solve this problem? (*If needed:* Who can think of a DIFFERENT way for Dilly to get Poppy to let him have the toy?)

And what else?

Elicit and write alternative solutions on the chalkboard in the usual way, then ask two different children to devise and act out another problem with the puppets. Let them know they can talk this time if they want to. After they have acted out the problem:

(To the group) Can you guess what the problem is?

What can Dilly and Poppy do to solve this problem?

What else?

Elicit and write alternative solutions.

A Story

PURPOSE

To encourage generation of more alternative solutions and help children see that they do not need to give up too soon, as well as to review ICPS feeling words

MATERIALS

Any storybook that presents an interpersonal problem

Feeling face stickers or chalkboard

TEACHER SCRIPT

I'm going to read a story, but first I want to pretend a problem.

Hold the book up as if to read it to the group.

(Child 1), come up and stand right in front of this book so those behind you can NOT see.

OK, who can think of something to do OR say so (Child 1) will sit down? *(Let children respond.)*

That's *one* way. (Child 1), keep standing.

Now try to think of lots of DIFFERENT ways to solve this problem.

Elicit alternative solutions in the usual way. Classify enumerations or have children classify them. Continue until children can generate no further solutions.

Now I'm really going to read the story.

Read the story. If necessary, reread. At appropriate points, ask the following questions:

What happened? What's the problem?

Does anyone see a DIFFERENT problem? (*If yes:* Let's choose *one* problem to talk about.)

How do you think (Character 1) felt when _____?
(Repeat the problem.)

Do you think (Character 2) felt the SAME way OR
a DIFFERENT way?

What did (Character 1) do or say to solve the problem?

How did (Character 2) feel when (Character 1) did or said that?

Did (Character 1) pick a good time or NOT a good time to do or say that?

Could (Character 1) have tried a DIFFERENT way to solve this problem? Any other ideas?

Next ask the following questions to help children review feeling words:

Did anyone do something to make someone in the class feel HAPPY today?

(To the child who performed the action) Tell us about it.

(To the recipient of the action) Did that make you feel HAPPY?

If the action made the recipient feel happy, have the child who performed the action give the recipient a happy feeling face sticker or draw a happy feeling face on the chalkboard.

Did anyone do something today to make someone feel SAD, ANGRY, or AFRAID?

Tell us about it.

Was the problem solved?

If yes: How did you two feel BEFORE the problem was solved?

If no: How did you try to solve the problem?

What happened when you did that?

What else can you do to solve this problem?

Have the child who performed the action choose the appropriate feeling face sticker or draw the feeling face on the chalkboard. If the problem was solved:

How did you feel AFTER the problem was solved?

Have the child who performed the action give the recipient a happy feeling face sticker or draw a happy feeling face on the chalkboard.

HINT

If during the first part of the lesson a child really is in the way while you read a story, ask the group for ideas to solve this problem. If hitting or pushing is suggested, ask, "How MIGHT _____ feel if you do that?" After the response, ask, "Can you think of a DIFFERENT way?"

ICPS Tic-Tac-Toe

PURPOSE

To give children practice in generating solutions and identifying enumerations

MATERIALS

Chalkboard or easel

TEACHER SCRIPT

Today we're going to play the game tic-tac-toe in a special way. But first, as a warm-up, we'll play it the regular way.

Who knows how to play this game?

Draw a tic-tac-toe box on the chalkboard. If anyone does not know how to play, demonstrate or have a student explain the game. Pick two children and have them play the game in the usual way.

OK. Now we're going to play this game in a new way.

I'm going to tell you a problem.

The *X* person thinks of lots of solutions, one for each box.

The *O* person thinks of lots of solutions, too.

Each person takes a turn picking a box and giving a solution.

If the person gives a DIFFERENT solution, he or she gets to put an *X* or *O* in the box.

If the person gives a solution like one that was already given, he or she sits down and another player gets a chance.

If the new player gives a DIFFERENT solution, he or she can then pick the SAME or a DIFFERENT box.

As soon as we put a solution in the box, the rest of you watch and try to catch solutions that are kind of the SAME.

Choose two children to come up and play the game. If necessary, remind the group that the object of the game is to be the first one to get three Xs or Os in a line.

Here's the problem: Jack was playing with Tim's new wooden model airplane and broke it.

He's afraid Tim will be ANGRY.

What can Jack do or say so Tim won't be ANGRY?

Draw a big tic-tac-toe box and write down the player's solutions in the squares of their choosing. If the solution is an original one, let the player mark an X or O, as the example shows.

Glue it X		*Fix it* *(Enumeration)*
Say sorry X	Buy a new one O	
Give him candy O		

If an enumeration is offered, write it down and wait for a child to catch it. If a child catches it, ask how the solution is "kind of the SAME" as another, then erase the enumeration. (In the sample provided, "Fix it" is an enumeration of "Glue it" and should be erased.) The child who catches the enumeration replaces the child who gave it. If the new player can give a different solution, he or she can pick the same or a different square.

If a child does not catch the enumeration, say, "Oh, we have two solutions here that are kind of the SAME. Who can tell me WHY they're kind of the SAME?" If you point out the enumeration, let the original players continue.

HINT

If a child's response is seemingly irrelevant, ask, "How will that help keep Tim from being ANGRY?" If the response is still irrelevant, erase the idea and ask for a new solution.

Poppy and Dilly, Part I

PURPOSE

To encourage role-play of problem solutions

MATERIALS

Any two hand puppets (for example, Poppy the Pup and Dilly the Duck)

TEACHER SCRIPT

If going to the teacher does not happen frequently in your classroom, adapt the following statement so that it refers to children in another classroom.

We're having a problem in this room and I need ALL of you to help me solve it.

Every day you tell me about the problems that you are having with one another.

Telling me is *one* way to solve problems, but I know you can think of DIFFERENT ways.

Poppy and Dilly are here to show you what I mean.

Dilly:	Teacher, Poppy poked me in the eye.
Poppy:	I did not—you poked *me* in the eye.
Teacher:	What happened BEFORE anyone got poked in the eye?
Dilly:	I was standing in line to come inside, and Poppy poked me in the eye with her jacket.
Poppy:	Did not!
Teacher:	Poppy, what do you think happened?
Poppy:	I was putting on my jacket, and it flew up when I went to put it on, and it hit Dilly. Then Dilly poked me in the eye. It really hurt.
Teacher:	Did you try to hurt Dilly?
Poppy:	No.
Teacher:	Dilly, how do you feel now?
Dilly:	ANGRY.

Teacher:	And Poppy, how do you feel?
Poppy:	FRUSTRATED.
Teacher:	What is something you can do so Dilly is NOT ANGRY and Poppy is NOT FRUSTRATED? How can we solve this problem?
Dilly:	Tell the teacher.
Teacher:	That's *one* way. Can you think of a DIFFERENT way? A way to solve this problem yourselves?
Dilly:	We could talk it out.
Poppy:	OR we could be friends.
Dilly:	OR we could give each other presents.
Poppy:	*(To the group)* What else could we do?

Let children act out some of the solutions they suggest, taking turns holding the puppets.

HINT

Use puppets to role-play actual problems that come up in the classroom or that a child reports to you. If desired, place feeling face stickers on the tip of a tongue depressor to make little puppets that children can keep at their desks and use for role-playing.

Finding More Solutions

MINI-DIALOGUE

Situation: Rhoda wants to join others in play.

Rhoda: *(To a group playing dolls)* Can I be the mommy?

Elaine: No! I'm the mommy!

Rhoda: *(Pouts and starts to walk away.)*

Teacher: What's the matter?

Rhoda: I want to be the mommy.

Teacher: Do you want to be the mommy OR do you want to play with those children?[1]

Rhoda: Play with the children.

Teacher: Can you think of something DIFFERENT you can do or say so they will let you play?[2]

Rhoda: No.

Teacher: How can you find out what they would like? Do you remember the Do You Like Game?[3]

Rhoda: *(To the children)* Do you like oranges?

Elaine: Yeah!

Rhoda: I'll be the orange lady! OK?

Elaine: OK.

NOTES

[1] The teacher helps the child identify the real problem.

[2] The teacher guides the child to think of alternative solutions.

[3] The teacher refers to the Do You Like Game (see Lesson 23).

CONSEQUENCES

The lessons in this section help children understand the possible consequences of a particular solution. A *consequence* is a reaction by Person B in direct relationship to an act performed by Person A. For example, if Sally hits Megan, Megan might, in consequence, choose to hit her back, tell the teacher, or not play with her anymore.

Lessons 61 through 66 help children learn to understand the sequence of events. Lesson 67 helps children examine whether an idea is or is not a good one, for early evaluation of solutions to interpersonal problems. Understanding of these ideas is prerequisite to actual consequential thinking, which, along with other related concepts, is taught in Lessons 68 through 74. The goal of consequential thinking is to help children think about what might happen next if a particular solution were carried out.

To this point, the exchanges between children and teacher have been "mini-dialogues," including some but not all of the steps in full ICPS dialoguing. After Lesson 68, in which true consequential thinking is first taught, you may begin to conduct full ICPS dialoguing in the classroom. Basically, this involves asking children "What MIGHT happen next" in addition to using the steps already described. Examples of full ICPS dialogues appear after Lesson 74.

PROCEDURE

As shown in the lessons, you can elicit consequences by undertaking the following steps:

1. State the problem or have the child state the problem.

2. Elicit alternative solutions in the usual way.

3. When a solution conducive to asking for consequences comes up, use that one. (Usually, "hit," "grab," or "tell someone" are good ones to start with.)

4. Write this solution on the left side of chalkboard or easel.

5. Say, "OK, let's make up a DIFFERENT kind of story. Pretend the child *(repeat the solution)*. What MIGHT happen next in the story?" Be sure to elicit direct consequences only, not *chain reactions*. For instance, if Sally hits Megan, Sally may continue a chain of events: Megan might hit Sally back (a direct consequence), then Sally might throw a block at her. Sally's throwing the block is a chain reaction to hitting back, not the direct consequence of Sally's first hitting Megan. If chaining occurs, point it

out. For instance, you could say, "That MIGHT happen if Megan hits Sally back. What MIGHT happen next when Sally first hits Megan?"

6. Say, "Let's think of lots of things that MIGHT happen next if *(repeat solution)*. I'm going to write all the things that MIGHT happen next on the board. Let's fill up the whole board." Write these consequences in a column on the right side of the board and draw arrows from the solution to them, as the example shows.

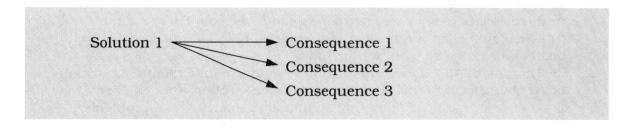

7. If necessary, probe for further consequences by asking, "What MIGHT _____ say? What MIGHT _____ do?"

8. Evaluate both positive solutions as well as negative ones. Occasionally ask, "What could _____ do so (a particular negative consequence) will NOT happen?"

ENUMERATIONS

As they do when asked for alternative solutions, children often give consequences that are variations on a theme. Classify these responses in the same way you would solutions, pointing out that the ideas are all "kind of the SAME." Ask for "something that MIGHT happen that is DIFFERENT" from the enumerated response.

UNCLEAR OR APPARENTLY IRRELEVANT RESPONSES

Handle unclear or seemingly irrelevant responses in the same way as for alternative solutions. Find out what the child has in mind. When eliciting consequences, it is especially important to question the child as to who is doing the action. For example, if a boy wants a girl to let him feed their pet hamsters, the response "grab the food" could be either solution or consequence. If the boy grabs the food, it could be a solution to his problem. If the girl grabs the food, it could be a consequence to whatever solution is proposed. If the child means that the boy grabs the food (a solution), you can elicit a consequence by asking, "What MIGHT the girl do or say if the boy does that?"

Mystery Sequence

PURPOSE

To help children think sequentially, a precursor to anticipating what MIGHT happen next

MATERIALS

Illustrations 25–28

TEACHER SCRIPT

Today's ICPS game is called Mystery Sequence.

We're going to use the words BEFORE and AFTER.

I'm going to show you some pictures, and you tell me what happens first, what happens second, what happens third, and what happens fourth.

Let's see if you remember what BEFORE and AFTER mean.

Everybody stand up.

Now jump.

Did you stand up BEFORE or AFTER you jumped?

Show children Illustrations 25–28. Place them out of sequence on the ledge of a chalkboard or on a table.

Look at these pictures carefully. They are NOT what would really happen first, second, third, and fourth.

Who knows what would happen first?

(To the child who responds) Come up and put the picture that shows what would happen first here.

Now second.

Now third.

Now fourth.

Point to the position farthest left for the first illustration, then to the spots immediately to the right for the next three. Three sequences are possible:

Sequence 1

1. The boy saves money in his piggy bank. (Illustration 25)
2. The boy sees the big wheels in the store. (Illustration 26)
3. The boy gets money out of his piggy bank. (Illustration 27)
4. The boy rides away on the big wheels he bought. (Illustration 28)

Sequence 2

1. The boy saves money in his piggy bank. (Illustration 25)
2. The boy gets money out of his piggy bank. (Illustration 27)
3. The boy sees the big wheels in the store. (Illustration 26)
4. The boy rides away on the big wheels he bought. (Illustration 28)

Sequence 3

1. The boy sees the big wheels in the store. (Illustration 26)
2. The boy saves money in his piggy bank. (Illustration 25)
3. The boy gets money out of his piggy bank. (Illustration 27)
4. The boy rides away on the big wheels he bought. (Illustration 28)

After the child has placed the illustrations in order:

Tell us what happens.

If incorrect: Could the boy (for example, ride the big wheels out of the store BEFORE paying for it)?

IF the boy rides the big wheels out of the store BEFORE paying for it, THEN what MIGHT happen next?

If still needed: Can someone else help us?

After a sequence is given, invite other children to suggest alternative sequences and/or to speculate on what might have happened between the steps shown in the illustrations. For example:

The boy saved his money.

Then he saw the big wheels in the store.

What could have happened AFTER he saved his money and BEFORE he got to the store? It can be something NOT shown in a picture.

What could have happened AFTER he got the money out of his piggy bank and BEFORE he rode away on the big wheels?

ILLUSTRATION 25   Lesson 61

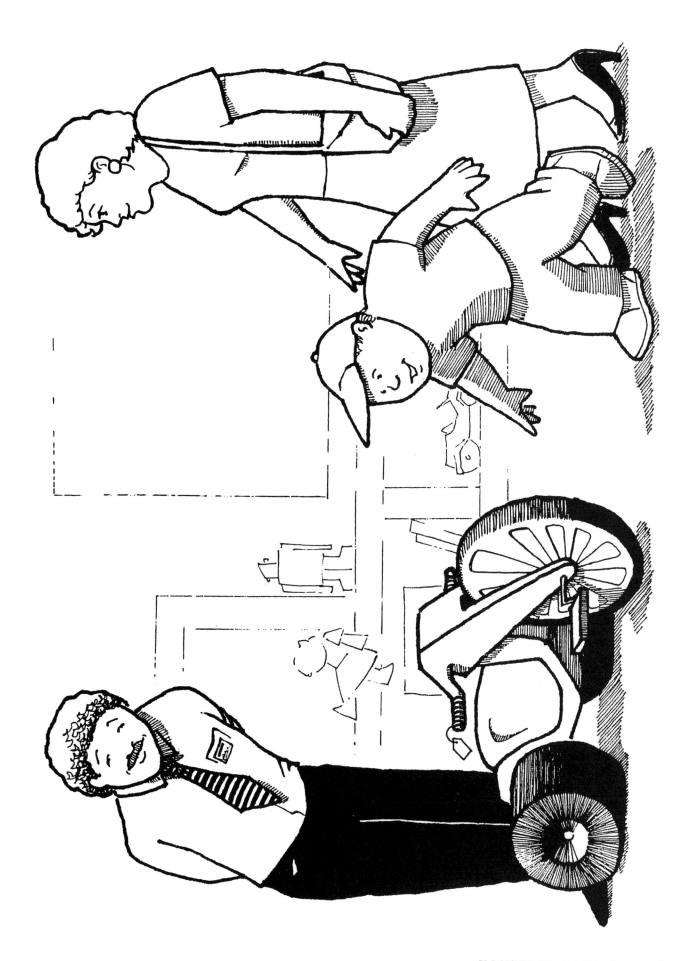

ILLUSTRATION 26   Lesson 61

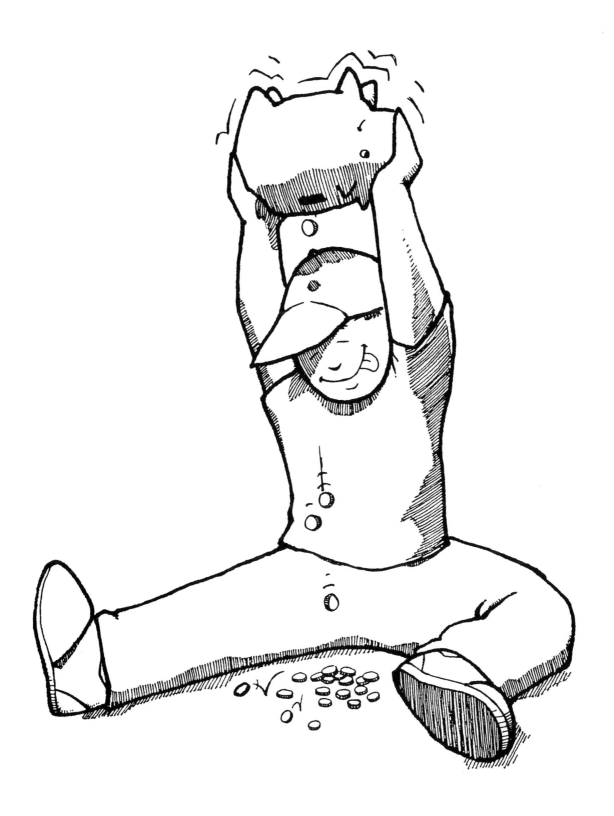

ILLUSTRATION 27   Lesson 61

ILLUSTRATION 28   Lesson 61

Story Continuation

PURPOSE

To review feeling words and strengthen understanding of sequencing

MATERIALS

Chalkboard or easel

TEACHER SCRIPT

Today I want you to make up a story about kids.

In your story, use at least three of these feeling words.

Write the following feeling words on the chalkboard: happy, sad, angry, afraid, proud, frustrated, impatient, worried, *and* relieved.

In your story, also think of a problem and how it will be solved.

Ask a child to start the story. After a few sentences, let the first child stop and ask another child, "Then what happens?" Write the story on the board as it unfolds. Continue until the problem in the story has been solved. When the story is over, ask what happened before and after specific events.

Interpersonal Mystery Sequence

PURPOSE

To strengthen understanding of sequencing by focusing on an interpersonal problem

MATERIALS

Illustrations 29–32

TEACHER SCRIPT

Show children Illustrations 29–32. Place them out of sequence on the ledge of a chalkboard or on a table.

Here are some more pictures, but the story is out of order.

Who knows what happened first?

Come up and put the picture that would happen first here.

What second?

And third?

And fourth?

Point to the position farthest left for the first illustration, then to the spots immediately to the right for the next three. Three sequences are possible:

Sequence 1

1. The boy knocks down the snowman. (Illustration 29)
2. The boy helps rebuild the snowman. (Illustration 30)
3. The boy helps finish rebuilding the snowman. (Illustration 31)
4. The boy and girl admire the snowman. (Illustration 32)

Sequence 2

1. The boy and girl admire the snowman. (Illustration 32)
2. The boy knocks down the snowman. (Illustration 29)
3. The boy helps rebuild the snowman. (Illustration 30)
4. The boy helps finish rebuilding the snowman. (Illustration 31)

Sequence 3

1. The boy helps build the snowman. (Illustration 30)

2. The boy helps finish building the snowman. (Illustration 31)

3. The boy and girl admire the snowman. (Illustration 32)

4. The boy knocks down the snowman. (Illustration 29)

After each sequence is given, ask for another possible order. Invite children to say what happened before and after each step. The following questions may help:

Did the boy knock the snowman down BEFORE or AFTER they built it?

WHY do you think he knocked it down?

WHY else?

What could have happened AFTER he knocked the snowman down? It can be something NOT shown in a picture.

Can anyone think of a still DIFFERENT way the story could go? Something else that MIGHT have happened first?

ILLUSTRATION 29 Lesson 63

ILLUSTRATION 30 Lesson 63

ILLUSTRATION 31 Lesson 63

ILLUSTRATION 32 Lesson 63

My ICPS Book, Part IV

PURPOSE

To show children how to express the sequence of an interpersonal problem by drawing it

MATERIALS

Crayons and paper

Children's ICPS folders

TEACHER SCRIPT

Today we're going to draw a problem—something that happened to you and another kid, or you and me, or you can just make it up.

First tell me what the problem is.

Circulate and write down the problems as children dictate them. If children can print, they may choose to write their own captions, as the sample drawings, done by a 6-year-old, show.

Drawing 1

Now tell me the very first thing that started the problem.

OK, draw that first. Draw the very first thing that happened.

Show in your drawing how each person felt.

Drawing 2

What was the next thing that happened?

OK, draw that on another page.

Drawing 3

How can this problem be solved?

Draw on another page what the people can do to solve the problem.

When finished, encourage each child to show his or her drawings to the group. Ask each child the following questions:

Can you tell us what happened first? (Drawing 1)

What was the next thing that happened? (Drawing 2)

How did the problem get solved? (Drawing 3)

What do you think MIGHT happen AFTER the people solve the problem?

What else could they have done to solve this problem?
(*If needed, to the group:* Does anyone else know a DIFFERENT way to solve this problem?)

(*To the child*) Which way do you like better? The one you drew or the other one?

WHY?

Be sure to save children's drawings in their ICPS folders or put some up for display.

SAMPLE DRAWINGS: PROBLEM SEQUENCE

Drawing 1: Ollie and Tippy are fighting over candy.

Drawing 2: Ollie snatches the candy, and the stick breaks off it. Ollie gets the stick. Tippy gets the candy.

A Big Problem

Ollie-stick   Tippy-candy

Drawing 3: We'll all share the candy.

The problem is solved
mom   mom says we all have
candy.
ollie   Tippy

Uh-Oh, They're Fighting

PURPOSE

To help children understand the reasons behind a particular event

MATERIALS

Illustration 33
Chalkboard or easel

TEACHER SCRIPT

Show children Illustration 33.

> Uh-oh. These boys are fighting.
>
> I wonder WHY they're fighting.
>
> Can you tell me WHY? *(Let children respond.)*
>
> That's *one* BECAUSE (reason).
>
> Let's think of lots of BECAUSES (reasons).
>
> I'll write all your reasons on the chalkboard.

Encourage children to come up with as many reasons as they can, writing each one on the board. Continue until no more reasons are given, then pick one—for example, one boy broke the other's airplane.

> Let's go back even BEFORE this boy *(point)* broke the other boy's *(point)* airplane.
>
> What MIGHT have happened BEFORE he did that?
>
> You know, WHY did one boy break the other boy's plane?
>
> RESPONSE: BECAUSE he laughed at him.
>
> OK. This boy *(point)* MIGHT have laughed at the other boy *(point)*.
>
> And WHY did this boy laugh?
>
> RESPONSE: BECAUSE the other boy spilled paint on his pants.

OK. Let's start with that.

How MIGHT he have spilled paint on his pants?

Then how MIGHT the boy have felt?

And how MIGHT his mother have felt?

OK, then the other boy laughed at him.

Was that a good idea?

What happened AFTER the other boy laughed at him?

He broke the other boy's airplane.

Generate alternative solutions to the problem in the usual way, writing children's suggestions on the board.

ILLUSTRATION 33 Lesson 65

Dealing With Fighting

MINI-DIALOGUE

Situation: Raymond and Tony are fighting.

Teacher:	*(To both)* What happened? What's the matter?[1]
Raymond:	Tony hit me.
Tony:	He hit me first.
Raymond:	I did not.
Teacher:	Do you two see what happened the SAME way or a DIFFERENT way?
Raymond:	A DIFFERENT way.
Teacher:	*(To Tony)* What happened BEFORE you two started fighting?[2]
Tony:	He called me stupid!
Teacher:	*(To Raymond)* Is that WHY Tony hit you?[3]
Raymond:	Yeah.
Teacher:	*(To Raymond, in a nonthreatening voice)* WHY did you call Tony stupid?
Raymond:	I don't know.
Teacher:	*(To both)* Fighting is *one* thing you can do. Can you think of something to do that is DIFFERENT from fighting?[4]
Tony:	*(To Raymond)* Don't call me stupid.
Raymond:	*(Shakes Tony's hand.)*

NOTES

[1] The teacher elicits the children's view of the problem.

[2] The teacher does not focus on finding out who really hit whom first. (He'll never know anyway.) Instead, he guides children to think of the sequence of events in preparation for consequential thinking.

[3] The real problem begins to be identified.

[4] The teacher helps the children solve the problem for themselves.

A Story

PURPOSE

To enhance story comprehension and integrate ICPS concepts presented thus far

MATERIALS

Any storybook that includes an interpersonal problem

TEACHER SCRIPT

Read the story. Reread, if necessary. Use the suggested questions as appropriate.

Determine the Problem

What happened?

What's the problem in this story?

Identify the Sequence of Events

Who remembers what happened BEFORE _____?
(Describe the problem in the story.)

The problem probably happened BECAUSE _____.

Identify Characters' Feelings

How does (Character 1) feel?

Does (Character 2) feel the SAME way OR a DIFFERENT way?

Identify Characters' Solutions

What did _____ do to solve the problem?

Anything else?

Generate More Alternative Solutions

What else could the people have done to solve the SAME problem?

Any other ideas?

If, for example, someone in the story is bossy or brags, you can ask questions like the following:

How do people feel when someone is bossy?

Do you know WHY someone MIGHT be bossy?

Do you know a DIFFERENT BECAUSE?

Can you think of a time someone in the story was bossy?

What did _____ say or do that was bossy?

Can anyone else think of a DIFFERENT time?

How about bragging?

What did _____ say or do that was bragging?

WHY do you think someone MIGHT brag?

Can you think of a DIFFERENT way to _____?
(Repeat the reason given.)

Is That a Good Idea?

PURPOSE

To encourage early consequential thinking

MATERIALS

Illustration 34

TEACHER SCRIPT

Before we talked about good times and NOT good times to ask or do something.

Now we're going to talk about good ideas and NOT good ideas.

Give each child a copy of Illustration 34.

Look at these pictures carefully.

(To the group) Find someone who is doing something that you think IS a good idea. Just pick one. *(Show one finger.)*

Put the number 1 on the line under the picture.

If children cannot write numbers, call on a child to tell you which illustration he or she chose.

(Child 1), tell us what the child in the picture you chose is doing.

WHY is that a good idea? What MIGHT happen next?

How MIGHT the child feel if that happens?

Do you think the child would feel that way BEFORE or AFTER (he/she) _____? *(For example:* Brushed her teeth, shared his toy.)

(If the illustration includes a second child) How MIGHT the other child feel if that happens?

(To the group) Who else thinks what is happening in this picture IS a good idea?

WHY do you think that?

If you think that IS a good idea, raise your hand.

Those of you who have your hands up feel the SAME way about this.

Does anyone think that is NOT a good idea?

WHY do you think that?

Anyone else?

Do you have a DIFFERENT reason, a DIFFERENT BECAUSE?

If you think what is happening in this picture is NOT a good idea, raise your hand.

If no one raises a hand: ALL of you think the SAME way about this picture. You ALL think what is happening in this picture IS a good idea.

If one or more raise hands: SOME of you think that what is happening in this picture IS a good idea. SOME of you think it is NOT a good idea. DIFFERENT people think DIFFERENT ways about the SAME thing.

(To the group) Find someone who is doing something that you think is NOT a good idea.

Write the number 2 on the line under the picture.

(Child 2), tell us what the child is doing.

WHY is that NOT a good idea? What MIGHT happen next?

How MIGHT the child feel if that happens?

Would the child feel that way BEFORE or AFTER (he/she) _____?
(For example: Burned herself, laughed at the other child.)

(If the illustration includes a second child) How MIGHT the other child feel?

What could the child do that IS a good idea?

Then what MIGHT happen next?

(To the group) Who else thinks what is happening in the picture is NOT a good idea?

WHY do you think that?

Can you think of a DIFFERENT reason, a DIFFERENT BECAUSE?

If you think what is happening in the picture IS a good idea, raise your hand.

WHY do you think that IS a good idea?

Anyone else?

WHY do you think that?

If children are in agreement: ALL of you think the SAME way. You ALL think what is happening in this picture IS a good idea.

If one or more disagree: SOME of you think what is happening in this picture IS a good idea. SOME of you think it is NOT a good idea. DIFFERENT people think DIFFERENT ways about the SAME thing.

We talked about *(describe the first picture discussed)* as a good idea.

Who put the number 1 under a DIFFERENT picture? A picture of a DIFFERENT child doing something you think IS a good idea?

Repeat the previous line of questioning for other pictures illustrating something that IS a good idea.

We talked about *(describe the second picture discussed)* as NOT a good idea.

Who put the number 2 under a DIFFERENT picture? A picture of a DIFFERENT child doing something you think is NOT a good idea?

Repeat the previous line of questioning for other pictures illustrating something that is NOT a good idea.

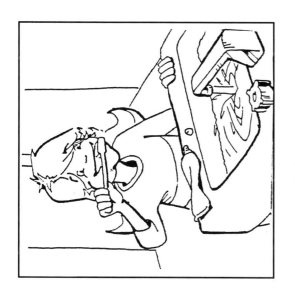 

ILLUSTRATION 34   Lesson 67

Is That a Good Idea?

The following examples show how guiding the child to focus on alternate behaviors can help avoid arguments, counterarguments, and simple power plays between teacher and child.

SOME HELPFUL QUESTIONS

When a child is running inside:

Is running inside a good idea?

What MIGHT happen next?

How will you feel if that happens?

What can you do that IS a good idea?

When a child is drawing on a desk:

Is drawing on your desk a good idea?

What can you draw on that IS a good idea?

When a child is talking inappropriately during a lesson:

Is talking during a lesson a good idea if I do NOT want you to talk?

How do think I feel when you do that?

When IS a good time to talk?

When a child is pushing in line:

Is pushing in line a good idea?

How MIGHT _____ feel if you push (him/her)?

What MIGHT happen next?

Would that happen BEFORE or AFTER you pushed (him/her)?

How would you feel if that happens?

What can you do so that will NOT happen?

If a child says something is not a good idea because of an external reason, such as punishment, ask, "What else MIGHT happen next?" Try to get the child to focus on internal reasons—for example, "He might get hurt" or "It might break."

MINI-DIALOGUES

Situation 1: Erika's hand is near the blades of the egg-beater as she is mixing soap flakes and water.

Teacher: Is that a good place for your hand?

Erika: No, BECAUSE I MIGHT get hurt.

Erika takes hold of the handle. No more needs to be said.

Situation 2: Sam is standing under a swing another child is on.

Teacher: *(Pulls Sam away gently.)* Was that a good place to stand?

Sam: No.

Teacher: What MIGHT happen if you stand under a swing like that?

Sam: I'd get hit.

Teacher: How would you feel if you got hit?

Sam: SAD.

Teacher: Can you think of a DIFFERENT place to stand so you won't get hit and won't feel SAD?

Sam: Over there. *(Points to a safe place.)*

Note that the teacher first removes Sam from the situation because he is in danger of getting hurt, then uses ICPS dialoguing.

Situation 3: Linwood is tying his rope to a gate where people are trying to enter.

Teacher: Linwood, is that a good place to tie your rope?

Linwood: Yes.

Teacher: Can people get in if the gate is tied up?

Linwood: No.

Teacher: Can you think of a DIFFERENT place to tie your rope?

The teacher recognizes that the child's goal is to tie the rope, not to prevent others from entering.

What Might Happen Next? Part I

PURPOSE

To illustrate that what we do and say affects what others do and say

MATERIALS

Illustration 35

Chalkboard or easel

TEACHER SCRIPT

NOTE

After this lesson, you may integrate full ICPS dialoguing in the classroom. Examples appear following Lesson 74.

Show children Illustration 35.

Let's pretend the problem here is that this girl on top of the slide *(point)* wants to come down, and the boy at the bottom *(point)* won't get off.

What can the girl do or say so the boy will get off?

I'm going to put ALL your solutions on the left side of the chalkboard.

Elicit three or four solutions. Write each one as given, as the following example shows.

1. She could push him off.
2. She could say, "Get off!"
3. She could tell his mother.

OK, listen carefully.

Let's talk about the idea to push the boy off.

IF the girl pushes him off, THEN what MIGHT happen next?

I'm going to write what MIGHT happen next here. *(Indicate the right side of the board.)*

RESPONSE: He'll hit (punch, kick) her. *(Write this consequence on the right side of the board. Very dramatically, draw an arrow as shown.)*

1. She could push him off. ⟶ 1. He'll hit (punch, kick) her.

OK, he MIGHT hit her. That's *one* thing that MIGHT happen. What else MIGHT happen?

Elicit as many consequences as possible, adding them to the list as given and drawing arrows from the solution as shown.

1. She could push him off.
   1. He'll hit (punch, kick) her.
   2. He won't be her friend.
   3. He won't get off.
   4. He'll get mad.

Remember to classify enumerations as they come up—for example, "He'll punch her" and "He'll kick her" are enumerations of the first consequence given, "He'll hit her." Say, "Punching her and hitting her are kind of the SAME BECAUSE they are both hurting. What MIGHT happen next that is DIFFERENT from hurting?"

(When a number of consequences have been generated) Look at ALL the things that MIGHT happen just from this one act.

Who thinks pushing the boy off IS a good idea?

WHY?

Who thinks pushing him off is NOT a good idea?

WHY?

OK. Let's talk about way number two, "Say, 'Get off!' "

Help children generate possible consequences for other solutions if time and interest permit.

ILLUSTRATION 35   Lesson 68

What Might Happen Next? Part II

PURPOSE

To reinforce the idea that what we do and say affects what others do and say

MATERIALS

Illustration 36

Chalkboard or easel

TEACHER SCRIPT

Show children Illustration 36.

Let's talk about this picture.

WHY do you think this girl *(point)* is going to hit this boy *(point)*?

Elicit several possible problems, then pick one—for example, "The boy won't let the girl play with his toys."

So what is this girl's way of solving the problem, of making it better?

RESPONSE: The girl will hit the boy. *(Write this solution on the left side of the chalkboard.)*

Now listen carefully. IF the girl hits the boy, THEN what MIGHT happen next? *(If needed: What MIGHT the boy say or do?)*

RESPONSE: The boy will hit her back. *(Write this consequence on the right side of the board. Very dramatically, draw an arrow from the solution to it.)*

OK, the boy MIGHT hit the girl back.

I'm going to put that over here, on the right side of the board.

Let's think of lots of things that MIGHT happen next, AFTER the girl hits the boy.

Help children generate as many consequences as possible, adding them to the list as given and drawing arrows as shown in the example.

1. The girl will hit the boy. → 1. The boy will hit the girl back.
2. The boy will tell his mother (father, sister).
3. The boy will cry.

Who thinks hitting the boy to get the toys IS a good idea?

WHY?

Who thinks hitting the boy is NOT a good idea?

WHY?

If time permits, elicit a new solution and help children generate other possible consequences.

ILLUSTRATION 36   Lesson 69

Poppy and Dilly, Part II

PURPOSE

To give children additional practice in generating solutions and consequences

MATERIALS

Any two hand puppets (for example, Poppy the Pup and Dilly the Duck)

TEACHER SCRIPT

Teacher:	We have a problem here, and we really need the whole class to help solve it. What's wrong, Dilly and Poppy?
Poppy:	Dilly is sitting in my seat.
Teacher:	How do *you* see the problem, Dilly?
Dilly:	Poppy is sitting in *my* seat.
Teacher:	Do you two see this the SAME way or a DIFFERENT way?
Dilly and Poppy:	*(At the same time)* A DIFFERENT way.
Teacher:	OK, that means we have a problem to solve. How are you feeling, Poppy?
Poppy:	Mad, and I'm going to give him a bloody beak if he doesn't move.
Teacher:	*(To the group)* What MIGHT happen if Poppy punches Dilly in the nose?

Have the children name possible consequences—for example, "Dilly MIGHT (feel sad/get hurt/yell at Poppy"). After each relevant consequence, respond with, "That's one thing that MIGHT happen. Can you think of something else that MIGHT happen?"

Teacher:	*(To the group)* What is another way Poppy can get Dilly to let him have the seat so that Dilly does not have to (for example, feel sad/get hurt/yell at Poppy)?

Let children name more solutions. Pick one and elicit possible consequences.

HINT

When actual problems arise in the classroom (such as pushing in line, fighting for the same seat, and so forth), it is often effective to work on problem solving by role-playing with puppets. The puppets draw immediate and undivided attention and invite participation from all children.

How Can This Be?

PURPOSE

To illustrate that people may see the SAME situation in a DIFFERENT way

MATERIALS

Illustrations 37 and 38

TEACHER SCRIPT

Show children Illustration 37.

> This girl *(point)* just did her math lesson.
>
> How does she feel about her math lesson?
>
> *If needed:* HAPPY and _____. What's our big new word?
>
> *If still needed:* HAPPY and PROUD or HAPPY and FRUSTRATED?
>
> This boy *(point)* has the SAME lesson.
>
> How does he feel about it? (*If needed:* ANGRY and _____. What's our big new word?)
>
> Do they feel the SAME way or a DIFFERENT way about the math lesson?
>
> WHY MIGHT the girl feel PROUD about her lesson? BECAUSE _____.
>
> That's *one* BECAUSE.
>
> Who can think of a DIFFERENT BECAUSE?
>
> WHY MIGHT the boy feel FRUSTRATED about his math lesson? BECAUSE _____.
>
> That's *one* BECAUSE.
>
> Who can think of a DIFFERENT BECAUSE?

If a child names a feeling other than what you expect, ask why. He or she may have a relevant thought—for example, the boy might be frustrated because he can't do his math but feel proud for trying.

SOME of you MIGHT feel PROUD about math lessons.

SOME of you MIGHT feel FRUSTRATED.

Who feels PROUD about that?

(Child 1), WHY do you feel PROUD?

Who feels FRUSTRATED about math lessons?

(Child 2), WHY do you feel FRUSTRATED?

Do (Child 1) and (Child 2) feel the SAME way or a DIFFERENT way about math lessons?

Can DIFFERENT children feel DIFFERENT ways about the SAME thing?

Is it OK for DIFFERENT children to feel DIFFERENT ways about the SAME thing?

Next show children Illustration 38.

Do this boy *(point)* and this girl *(point)* feel the SAME way or a DIFFERENT way about the television show they're watching?

How do you think the girl feels?

How do you think the boy feels?

WHY MIGHT the boy feel (FRUSTRATED/ANGRY)? BECAUSE _____.

WHY MIGHT the girl feel HAPPY about the SAME television show?

What about television makes you feel HAPPY?

Does anyone ever feel ANGRY or FRUSTRATED when the television is on or a certain television show is on?

What did we learn from this? (*If needed:* In solving problems, people may feel a DIFFERENT way than you do about the SAME thing.)

Discuss other examples if time and interest permit.

ILLUSTRATION 37 Lesson 71

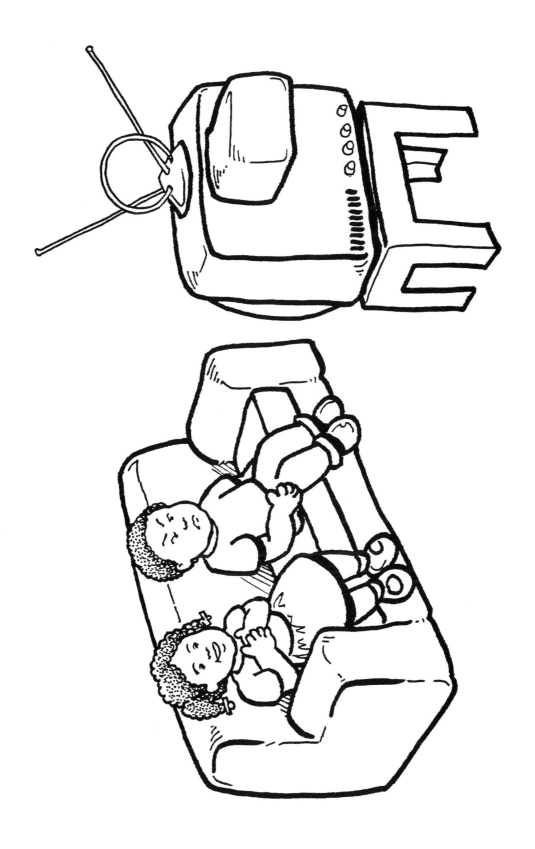

ILLUSTRATION 38 Lesson 71

Puppet Story: Would That Make You Happy?

PURPOSE

To review the idea that DIFFERENT people like DIFFERENT things and ways to find out others' preferences

MATERIALS

Any two hand puppets (for example, brother and sister puppets)

TEACHER SCRIPT

Brother: *(Cries.)*

Sister: *(To the group)* I wonder WHY my brother is so SAD? *(To brother)* WHY are you so SAD?

Brother: How do you know I'm SAD? How can you tell?

Sister: I can see with my eyes that you are crying.

Brother: I'm going to put my hands over your eyes. Now you can't see that I am crying. *(Does so.)*

Sister: I can still tell you're SAD.

Brother: *(Crying)* How?

Sister: I can hear you with my ears. *(Whispering, to the group)* I wonder WHY he's so SAD.

Brother: WHY do you think I'm so SAD?

Sister: BECAUSE you can't go out and play?

Brother: No, that's NOT WHY I'm so SAD.

Sister: MAYBE it's BECAUSE your friend did NOT come today.

Brother: No, that's NOT WHY I'm so SAD.

Sister: *(To the group)* Does anybody know WHY he is so SAD? MAYBE _____.

Ask three or four children for ideas.

Sister:	How can we find out? Let's ask together: "WHY are you so SAD?"
Brother:	BECAUSE I didn't get a star in school today.
Sister:	I wonder how I can make him feel better. *(Pauses, then, excitedly)* I think I know. Going to the zoo would make you HAPPY, right?
Brother:	No!
Sister:	No? Going to the zoo would make *me* HAPPY. I thought that would make you happy, too.
Brother:	I do like the zoo. But I went to the zoo BEFORE. I do NOT want to go again NOW.
Sister:	Oh, I didn't know you just went to the zoo. Would going for a walk make you HAPPY?
Brother:	No, I do NOT like to walk.
Sister:	Walking makes *me* happy. I thought walking would make you happy, too.
Brother:	DIFFERENT people like DIFFERENT things. You like to walk. I do NOT like to walk.
Sister:	*(To the group)* Do you have any ideas that MIGHT make my brother HAPPY? MAYBE _____.

Repeat each child's idea, then ask the child, "Would that make you HAPPY?" Then ask the brother puppet, "Would that make you HAPPY?" Have the brother sometimes agree and sometimes disagree. For example:

Sister:	*(If brother disagrees)* Candy makes *you* HAPPY. It does NOT make my brother HAPPY. Who has a DIFFERENT idea of what MIGHT make my brother HAPPY? *(If brother agrees)* Candy makes you AND my brother HAPPY.

Let children take turns holding the puppets and asking each other what makes them happy. Point out that it is fair for each child to have one turn.

HINT

Have the brother puppet agree with a more inhibited child's suggestion. Doing so will help the child gain confidence.

What Might Happen Next? Part III

PURPOSE

To reinforce the idea that what we do and say affects what others do and say

MATERIALS

Illustration 39

Chalkboard or easel

TEACHER SCRIPT

Show children Illustration 39.

Let's talk about this picture.

WHY do you think this boy *(point)* is pushing this other boy *(point)*?

Let children suggest a number of possible problems, then choose one.

So, what is this boy's way of solving this problem, of making it better?

RESPONSE: Pushing him off the bike. *(Write this solution on the left side of the chalkboard.)*

I'm going to write that this boy is pushing the other boy off his bike over here, on the left side of the board.

I'm going to write ALL the things that MIGHT happen next over here, on the right side.

What do you think MIGHT happen next if this boy pushes the other boy off the bike?

RESPONSE: The other boy will punch him. *(Write this consequence on the right side of the board. Very dramatically, draw an arrow from the solution to it.)*

That's *one* thing that MIGHT happen. The other boy MIGHT punch him.

The idea of this game is to think of lots of DIFFERENT things that MIGHT happen if this boy pushes the other boy off the bike.

What else MIGHT happen next?

Elicit as many consequences as possible, adding each to the list as given and drawing arrows as shown in the example.

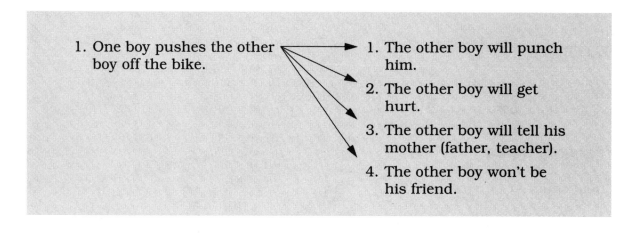

(When a number of consequences have been generated) Look at ALL the DIFFERENT things that MIGHT happen just from this one act, pushing the boy off the bike.

This boy pushed the other boy off the bike BECAUSE _____.

Who thinks pushing him off IS a good idea?

WHY do you think that?

Who thinks pushing him off is NOT a good idea?

WHY?

Who can think of a DIFFERENT way to get a chance to ride the bike?

RESPONSE: He could ask. *(Add this solution to the list on the left side of the board.)*

And what MIGHT happen if he tries that?

Elicit consequences for the new solution, as the example shows.

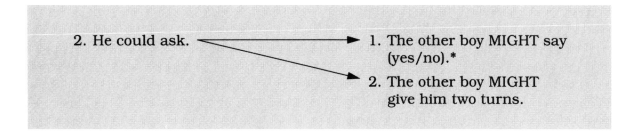

Be sure to elicit consequences of positive as well as negative solutions and remember to classify enumerations. Next ask the following questions:

> You may change your mind about what IS and what is NOT a good idea.
>
> Who NOW thinks pushing the boy off IS a good idea?
>
> Who NOW thinks pushing him off is NOT a good idea?
>
> Do ALL of you think the SAME way about this?
>
> Who thinks (for example, asking) IS a good idea?
>
> WHY?
>
> Who thinks asking is NOT a good idea?
>
> WHY?

HINT

Because both characters are boys, make sure you know which character the child means. If you're not sure, ask, "Who (says/does) that?" If the child is giving a solution, write it on the left side of the board; if a consequence, write it on the right.

---

* Kids have fun chanting, "He MIGHT say yes/he MIGHT say no" in response to the solution "He could ask."

ILLUSTRATION 39   Lesson 73

What Might Happen Next? Part IV

PURPOSE

To further reinforce the idea that what we do and say affects what others do and say

MATERIALS

Illustration 40

Chalkboard or easel

TEACHER SCRIPT

Show children Illustration 40.

What do you think this boy *(point)* is doing?

WHY do you think this boy *(point)* is pushing this other boy *(point)*?

Any other reason?

Let children suggest a number of possible problems, then choose one.

So, what is this boy's way of solving the problem, of making it better?

RESPONSE: Pushing in line. *(Write this solution on the left side of the chalkboard.)*

I'm going to write that this boy is pushing in line over here, on the left side of the board.

Now, what MIGHT happen next?

Elicit and write down possible consequences as given. Draw arrows as the example shows.

1. The boy pushes in line. ⟶ 1. Other kids will push back.
2. There will be a fight.
3. Someone will call him stupid.

If (for example, there is a fight), would that happen BEFORE or AFTER the boy pushes in line?

Is pushing in line a good idea? If you think yes, raise your hand.

WHY do you think that?

Who thinks pushing in line is NOT a good idea?

WHY?

When standing in line, what is NOT a good idea?

When standing in line, what IS a good idea?

Did anyone change his or her mind about whether pushing IS or is NOT a good idea?

Does anyone feel a DIFFERENT way about this NOW?

Do ALL of you feel the SAME way about this?

HINT

Leave this illustration on the wall or door where lines form. When a child really pushes, ask:

- What did we say about the boy in this picture?
- WHY did you push?
- What MIGHT happen next?
- What else can you do?

ILLUSTRATION 40 Lesson 74

ICPS Dialoguing

I WANT IT NOW

Non-ICPS Dialogue	**ICPS Dialogue**
(Teacher solves the problem)	(Child solves the problem)

Teacher:	Tanya, why did you snatch that doll from Janet?	Teacher:	What's the matter? What happened?[1]
Tanya:	'Cause she won't let me have it.	Tanya:	Janet won't give me the doll.
Teacher:	You can't grab. Why don't you ask her?[1]	Teacher:	How does that make Janet feel when you grab toys away from her?[2]
Tanya:	I did, and she said no!	Tanya:	Mad, but I don't care.
Teacher:	Why don't you try this puzzle?[2]	Teacher:	WHY do you have to have it back now?
Tanya:	I want the doll!	Tanya:	BECAUSE she's had a long turn.[3]
Teacher:	You should learn how to wait your turn. If you go around grabbing, no one will play with you.[3]	Teacher:	Grabbing is *one* thing you can do. What happened when you grabbed the doll?[4]
Tanya:	But she won't let me have it.	Tanya:	She grabbed it back and hit me.
Teacher:	I said no grabbing. Now say you're sorry.[4]	Teacher:	How did that make you feel?
Tanya:	*(To Janet)* I'm sorry.[5]	Tanya:	Mad.
		Teacher:	You're mad and Janet is mad, and Janet hit you. Can you think of a DIFFERENT way to get to play with the doll so you both won't be mad and so Janet won't hit you?[5]
		Tanya:	I could ask her.
		Teacher:	And what MIGHT happen then?[4]
		Tanya:	She'll say no.
		Teacher:	She MIGHT say no. What else can you think of to try if she says no?[5]
		Tanya:	I could say, "Let's play together."
		Teacher:	Good, you thought of two different ways.

NOTES

¹ Suggests a solution based on the assumption that grabbing is the problem. (In reality, grabbing is the child's solution to the problem of getting the doll.)

² Suggests an alternative activity, which, as predicted, the child refuses.

³ Still thinking for the child, this time telling her potential consequences.

⁴ Concerned only with teaching the child to wait, not with the child's perception of the problem.

⁵ A good way to get rid of a nagging adult.

¹ Elicits the child's view of the problem.

² Elicits the other child's feelings.

³ Now the teacher knows the real problem. The child would likely have felt frustrated if the teacher had focused on learning to wait. This child thought she had waited long enough.

⁴ Elicits consequences to both positive and negative actions.

⁵ Elicits alternative solutions.

IT'S MINE

Teacher:	What's the problem? What's wrong?	*Elicits the child's view of the problem.*
Nathan:	She never shares.	
Teacher:	What happened AFTER you did that?	*Encourages the child to think of consequences of his action.*
Nathan:	She cried.	
Teacher:	And how did Pam feel then?	*Elicits other's feelings.*
Nathan:	SAD.	
Teacher:	How do you feel about her NOT sharing?	*Elicits the child's own feelings.*
Nathan:	ANGRY!	
Teacher:	Grabbing is *one* thing you can do. Can you think of something DIFFERENT you can do so she won't be SAD and you won't be ANGRY?	*Helps the child think of alternative solutions.*
Nathan:	I can ask her.	
Teacher:	That's a DIFFERENT idea. Go ahead and try that.	
Nathan:	*(To Pam)* Can I have the blue crayon?	
Pam:	No!	
Teacher:	Oh, that idea did NOT work. Can you think of a second, new idea?	*Encourages the child not to give up too soon.*
Nathan:	*(To Pam)* I'll let you play with my new wagon.	
Pam:	OK.	
Teacher:	You thought of a DIFFERENT way. How do you feel about that?	

Adding Consequences

WHAT MIGHT HAPPEN IF . . .

Someone throws trash into the river?

What else?

Where IS a good place to throw trash?

No one waters the plants for 3 weeks?

No one feeds the fish?

No one walks the dog for 2 days?

A person takes drugs?

What else?

WHY would someone take drugs? BECAUSE _____.

What else could someone do to _____? *(Repeat the reason given.)*

George Washington's soldiers did NOT show up for battle?

Abraham Lincoln did NOT free the slaves?

The pilgrims did NOT land in America—they landed somewhere else?

Eighteen people sat in a canoe?

You ate 14 bags of potato chips, 10 boxes of candy, and 32 pieces of chocolate cake all at the SAME time?

I did not do ICPS with you?

MAKING CHOICES

Encourage consequential thinking in any area of the curriculum that deals with people who had choices, such as George Washington, Abraham Lincoln, or Martin Luther King. Ask the following questions:

What was the problem?

How do you think (he/she) felt about that?

What did (he/she) do to solve the problem?

WHY do you think (he/she) did that?

What happened when (he/she) did that?

What else MIGHT (he/she) have done to _____?
(Repeat reason or goal.)

SOLUTION-CONSEQUENCE PAIRS

The lessons in this section help teach children how to generate solution-consequence pairs. By doing so, children will ultimately be able to choose from among a number of solutions on the basis of their most likely consequences.

PROCEDURE

As shown in the lessons, the steps for teaching solution-consequence pairs are as follows:

1. State the problem or have the child state the problem.

2. Elicit one solution to the problem.

3. Ask for a consequence of that solution.

4. If the consequence is relevant, elicit a second solution.

5. Ask for the consequence of the second solution, and so on, as the example shows.

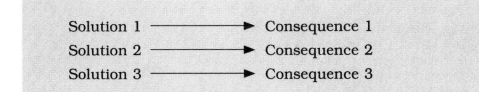

ENUMERATIONS AND UNCLEAR OR APPARENTLY IRRELEVANT RESPONSES

Treat enumerations and apparently irrelevant responses as you would for alternative solutions or consequences. Distinguish chain reactions from consequences if necessary.

What Might Happen If I Do That? Part I

PURPOSE

To introduce the idea of solution-consequence pairs and encourage immediate evaluation of problem solutions

MATERIALS

Illustration 41

Chalkboard or easel

TEACHER SCRIPT

Show children Illustration 41.

Let's pretend these two kids are at school, screaming at each other.

WHY are they screaming at each other? BECAUSE _____.

That's *one* BECAUSE.

Can you think of a DIFFERENT BECAUSE?

WHY else MIGHT they be screaming?

Classify enumerations—for example, screaming over a toy and over a crayon are both "screaming over something."

OK, let's start over.

How does this boy *(point)* see this problem? What does he think happened?

What does the girl think happened?

Do these kids see what happened the SAME way or a DIFFERENT way?

How does the girl feel?

How does the boy feel?

Now we're going to play a new game.

You tell me *one* thing the boy can do or say and *one* thing that MIGHT happen next if he does that.

I'm going to put your ideas over here on the left side of the chalkboard.

What could this boy do to (for example, get the crayon)?

RESPONSE: Ask for it. *(Solution—write this and other solutions as given on the left side of the board.)*

What MIGHT happen next?

I'm going to put what MIGHT happen next here on the right side of the board.

RESPONSE: She'll give it to him. *(Consequence—write this and other consequences as given on the right side of the board. Draw an arrow from solution to consequence, as the example shows.)*

1. He could ask for it.   ⟶   1. She'll give it to him.

Continue to elicit solution-consequence pairs as long as time and interest permit. Some possible responses are given in the following example.

1. He could ask for it. ⟶	1. She'll give it to him.
2. He could punch her (hit her, kick her). ⟶	2. She'll get hurt.
3. He could say, "I won't be your friend." ⟶	3. She won't care.
4. He could let her have his paints. ⟶	4. She'll let him use her crayon.
5. He could grab it. ⟶	5. She'll punch him.

HINT

Point dramatically to the boy when asking for a solution and to the girl when asking for a consequence. If a solution is seemingly irrelevant, ask how it might solve the problem. If a consequence is seemingly irrelevant, ask why that might happen next. The child may have something relevant in mind.

ILLUSTRATION 41   Lesson 75

What's That Problem? Part II

PURPOSE

To emphasize the importance of finding out what a problem is instead of making assumptions about it

MATERIALS

Illustration 42

Feeling face stickers

TEACHER SCRIPT

> **NOTE**
> Duplicate the feeling face drawings provided in Lesson 30, then cut them out or have children cut them out. Put a piece of double-stick tape on the back of each face. Alternatively, children may draw feeling faces.

Give each child a copy of Illustration 42 and one feeling face sticker for each emotion (a total of four). Instruct children to choose one sticker and put it on the face of the person they think has the problem. After they have done so, continue with the following questions:

(Child 1), who do you think has the problem in this picture?

What feeling face sticker did you choose?

(Child 2), who do you think has the problem here?

What feeling face sticker did you choose?

Oh, (Child 1) and (Child 2) saw (the SAME/a DIFFERENT) problem.

They chose (the SAME/a DIFFERENT) feeling face sticker(s).

Repeat with several other pairs of children.

SOME children saw the SAME person as having the problem.

ALL children did NOT see the SAME thing.

Looking at the SAME picture, DIFFERENT children saw
a DIFFERENT problem.

When we see people having a problem, do we know what the
problem is just by seeing with our eyes?

How can we find out what the problem really is?

Choose a problem identified by one of the children, then elicit solution-consequence pairs in the usual way.

ILLUSTRATION 42   Lesson 76

Imagine That

PURPOSE

To increase recognition that another might not know what happened if he or she did not see or hear it and to reinforce solution and consequence pairing

MATERIALS

Chalkboard or easel

TEACHER SCRIPT

Close your eyes.

Pretend I went out of the room.

While I was gone, (Child 1) took (Child 2's) pencil.

When I walked in, I saw (Child 2) hit (Child 1).

What MIGHT I think happened?

No matter what the response is, unless it is that you do not know, say:

No, I didn't see that.

What else MIGHT I think?

No matter what the response is, say:

How can I find out?

After asking is suggested as a way to find out, say:

What happened? What's really the problem? *(Let children respond.)*

Oh, I'm glad I asked you. I thought the problem was that (Child 2) hit (Child 1) BECAUSE that's all I saw.

I did NOT see what happened BEFORE (Child 2) hit (Child 1).

OK, it looks like the real problem was that (Child 1) wanted (Child 2's) pencil.

Next have children role-play the situation.

(Child 1) and (Child 2), come up here and show us the whole problem.

(Child 1), take (Child 2's) pencil.

(Child 2), show us what happened when (Child 1) took your pencil.

Remember, this is just a game. (*If needed:* Only pretend to hit him/her.)

(To Child 1) OK, taking the pencil is *one* way you can get (Child 2) to let you have it.

I'm going to put that idea over here on the left side of the chalkboard. *(Do so, as the example shows.)*

Now listen carefully. *(To Child 1)* What happened next when you took the pencil?

OK, (Child 2) hit you.

I'm going to put that idea over here on the right side of the board. *(Do so, drawing an arrow as the example shows.)*

1. Take it. ⟶ 1. (He/she) will hit.

(To the group) OK. How else could (Child 1) solve this problem?

What is something DIFFERENT (he/she) could do or say to get (Child 2) to let (him/her) have the pencil?

RESPONSE: Ask. *(Solution—add to the list.)*

And if (Child 1) asks, what MIGHT happen next?

RESPONSE: (He/she) MIGHT say yes. *(Consequence—add to the list.)*

Elicit additional solution-consequence pairs in the usual way, writing each on the board and drawing arrows as the example shows.

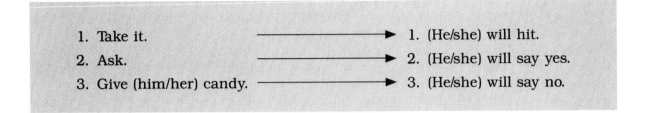

HINT

Make sure that, for solutions, children are referring to the first child; for consequences, to the second. If you are not sure, ask, "Who will do that?" If a child gives an irrelevant response (for example, saying "She will eat it" in response to the solution "Give her candy"), say, "Yes, that MIGHT happen," then ask, "What else MIGHT happen?" Try to elicit an interpersonal consequence. If needed, ask, "What might (Child 2) do or say next?"

Do I Know?

PURPOSE

To reinforce the idea that one needs information before being able to identify a problem

MATERIALS

Chalkboard or easel

Paper

TEACHER SCRIPT

NOTE

The help of a teacher aide or another adult is required for this lesson.

Remember when I pretended to go out of the room, and we had a pretend problem?

I didn't know (Child 1) took (Child 2's) pencil.

Today I'm *really* going to go out of the room.

While I'm gone, you think of a problem that kids MIGHT have with one another in school.

When I come back, I'm going to try to guess what the problem is.

Now _____ will help you while I'm gone.

But be very quiet BECAUSE it will be your secret.

The teacher aide or other adult should now help children choose a very "guessable" problem—for instance, pushing in line. He or she should then write the chosen problem on the chalkboard and cover it with a piece of paper.

> Aide: OK, let's practice the problem. *(To children needed to role-play the problem)* Come up front and *show* us the problem. No words. Just like before, when you showed us how to brush your teeth.

After the rehearsal, the aide should ask for a volunteer to tell you to come back into the room.

Aide: Does your teacher know what the problem is? You know what the problem is, but does your teacher know? *(To teacher)* _____, do you know what the problem is? Can you try to guess?

Teacher: Did the chairs walk away? *(Let children respond.)*

No? They have legs—they can walk. Did the sun come out at night?

I just do NOT know what the problem is. I have to find out. Who can *show* me so I can see with my eyes?

The aide should now have the children role-play the problem as they rehearsed it. You then try to guess the problem.

Oh, the problem is _____. *(For example:* _____ pushed someone in line.)

NOW I know what the problem is.

I did NOT ask.

I did NOT hear it with my ears.

What did I do? How did I find out?

Yes, I saw with my eyes.

Let children think of more silly problems like the ones you first guessed. If time and interest permit, ask children to think of another real problem; repeat the game with a different group of role-players.

What Might Happen If I Do That? Part II

PURPOSE

To further encourage immediate evaluation of problem solutions

MATERIALS

Illustration 43
Chalkboard or easel

TEACHER SCRIPT

Show children Illustration 43.

What is this boy doing?

RESPONSE: Taking the ball. *(Solution—write on the left side of the chalkboard.)*

WHY do you think he MIGHT be doing that?

WHY else?

Is that a good idea?

What MIGHT happen next? *(If needed:* What MIGHT the girl do or say?)

RESPONSE: She'll cry. *(Consequence—write on the right side of the board.)*

Listen again. I'm going to change the question.

Now tell me what else the boy could do to get to play with the ball.

Continue solution-consequence pairing, writing children's responses and drawing arrows as shown in the example. Investigate seemingly irrelevant solutions and consequences in the usual way.

1. He could take it.	⟶	1. She'll cry.
2. He could ask her.	⟶	2. She'll say (yes/no).
3. He could say, "Let's play catch."	⟶	3. They'll play together.

ILLUSTRATION 43   Lesson 79

What Else Can I Do?

PURPOSE

To help children sense whether or not a solution is successful

MATERIALS

Various classroom objects (for example, crayons, blocks, toys)

TEACHER SCRIPT

If you are working with a small group, give each child a different classroom object. Encourage the children to find ways to end up with the object desired. If you are working with a larger group, bring five children to the front and give each an object. In either case, if grabbing or hitting occurs, ask:

How does that make _____ feel? (*If needed:* HAPPY, SAD, or ANGRY?)

What MIGHT happen next if you grab or hit? (*If needed:* What MIGHT _____ do or say?)

What else can you do or say so (he/she) will give you the one you want?

If successful: How does that make you feel?

If not successful: Can you think of a DIFFERENT idea? (*If needed:* Can anyone else help think of something DIFFERENT?)

After each child ends up with the desired object, pick an object a child is holding and say, "Who is NOT holding _____?" If the child holding this object raises his or her hand, say to the child, "Listen carefully. Who is NOT holding _____?" Repeat with each object the children have, then ask each child, "What object do you NOT have?" Finally, alternate between do have and do NOT have.

Puppet Story: Reviewing Solutions

PURPOSE

To provide additional practice in generating alternative solutions

MATERIALS

Any two hand puppets (for example, Dilly the Duck and Poppy the Pup)

TEACHER SCRIPT

Have two children come up to the front. Give each a puppet, then have them role-play a simple problem. For example:

Dilly: We were both playing with these toys. I want you to help me put them away now.

Poppy: No. I don't want to.

Dilly: If you don't, I won't be your friend.

Teacher: Poppy, what do you say to that?

Poppy: I don't care.

Teacher: Oh, Dilly, you'll have to think of something DIFFERENT.

Dilly: I'll let you play with my toys.

Poppy: I don't like your toys.

Teacher: Dilly, what do you say to that?

When the child playing Dilly runs out of ideas, have another child come up and, as Dilly, offer other solutions for Poppy to respond to. Repeat with another problem if time and interest permit.

Asking Why

Asking why may diffuse an instigator's anger in a problem situation. In addition, it can reveal unexpected motivations. Encourage children to use this technique, illustrated in the following examples, whenever another child hits, pushes, chases, or name-calls.

Situation 1: Travis goes down the slide and runs into Adana, who is still at the bottom.

Adana: *(Crying)* Travis bumped me!

Teacher: Do you know WHY?

Adana: No.

Teacher: How can you find out?

Adana: *(To Travis)* I don't like that. WHY did you bump me?

Travis: I didn't see you.

Adana: Oh.

Travis: I'm sorry.

Situation 2: Linda appears sad and anxious.

Teacher: Linda, WHY are you so SAD?

Linda: Richard's chasing me.

Teacher: Do you know WHY?

Linda: No.

Teacher: How can you find out?

Linda: *(To Richard)* WHY are you chasing me?

Richard: I want to play with you.

Linda: You got nobody to play with?

Richard: Nope.

Linda: OK, I'll play with you.

Although the teacher might also have talked to Richard about DIFFERENT ways to get Linda's attention, this technique avoided a power play that might have occurred had the teacher said, "Richard, I can't let you chase Linda. Linda doesn't like to be chased." The problem was solved to the satisfaction of both children without stifling their thinking.

A Story

PURPOSE

To encourage story comprehension and integrate ICPS concepts

MATERIALS

Any storybook that concerns an interpersonal problem

TEACHER SCRIPT

Read the story to the class. If necessary, reread. At appropriate points, ask the following questions:

Identify the Problem

What happened? What's the matter?

What's the problem in this story?

What MIGHT have happened BEFORE the story started? Something that led up to the problem?

Identify Characters' Feelings

How do you think (Character 1) felt when that happened?

Do you think (Character 2) felt the SAME way OR a DIFFERENT way?

Identify Characters' Solutions

What did _____ (do/say) to solve the problem?

Anything else?

Did anyone else try to solve the SAME problem?

How?

Identify Consequences

What happened next AFTER _____? (Describe the solution.)

Was the solution tried at a good time or NOT a good time?

Was the solution a good idea or NOT a good idea?

WHY?

Generate New Solutions

What else MIGHT _____ have done to solve this problem?

Consider Consequences of the New Solution

Is that a good idea?

WHY?

Create a New Ending

How else MIGHT the story have ended?

Reread an earlier story, then ask additional questions. For example, to the sample story The Circus Baby *(see Lesson 53), you might ask the following:*

After: "But she was careful not to break anything."

Why is it a good idea NOT to break anything? BECAUSE _____?

After: "The bowl tipped and clattered off the table. Then Mr. Clown's stool gave a loud creak and split into many pieces."

How will Mr. and Mrs. Clown feel when they see this?

What MIGHT happen next? *(If needed:* What MIGHT they do or say?)

What could you do if you spilled everything on the floor?

What else could you do?

Is that a good idea? What MIGHT happen next?

WHY?

Let's see what happens in this story. *(Continue with the story.)*

Final Review

PURPOSE

To strengthen ICPS concepts taught thus far

MATERIALS

Illustrations 44–49

TEACHER SCRIPT

Throughout the lesson, keep discussion of illustrations at a fast pace. First show children Illustration 44.

Are ALL these children playing with the SAME OR DIFFERENT things?

(Child 1), which toy would you choose?

(To Child 1) Would (Child 2) choose the SAME toy OR a DIFFERENT one?

How can you find out?

Show children Illustration 45.

Are ALL these children near the fish bowl OR are SOME of them?

What MIGHT happen if this boy puts too much food in the water?

How MIGHT these kids feel if that happens?

Show children Illustration 46.

Each child has one cupcake.

If this child *(point to any pictured child)* takes a cupcake from another child *(point)*, how many cupcakes would the first child have?

How many would the second child have?

Is that FAIR?

WHY?

What MIGHT happen if one child takes a cupcake from another?

What else MIGHT happen?

What else can you think of that is NOT FAIR?

Show children Illustration 47.

What's happening in this picture?

Is this a good place to leave the skates?

What MIGHT happen if someone leaves roller skates at the top of the steps?

Can you think of a DIFFERENT place to put the skates so that will NOT happen?

Show children Illustration 48.

This child is interrupting these adults.

Do you know what *interrupting* means?

Is this a good time for this child to try to talk to the woman?

Can the woman talk to the child and the other person at the SAME time?

When IS a good time to talk to her?

What can the child do while she waits?

Show children Illustration 49.

What's happening in this picture?

Let's pretend both kids were playing, but the boy won't help the girl clean up.

Is that FAIR?

WHY?

How MIGHT the girl feel about that?

What can the girl do OR say so the boy will help her clean up?

What else?

ILLUSTRATION 44   Lesson 83

ILLUSTRATION 45   Lesson 83

ILLUSTRATION 46   Lesson 83

ILLUSTRATION 47 Lesson 83

ILLUSTRATION 48 Lesson 83

ILLUSTRATION 49   Lesson 83

APPENDIX A

Guidelines for Continued ICPS Teaching

Teaching does not stop once the formal ICPS lessons have been completed. If children are to associate how they think with what they do, you must continue to make frequent use of the ICPS dialoguing approach when interacting with children informally in the classroom. This association may be critical to how problem-solving thinking can guide behavior. It is also important to apply ICPS principles consistently whenever opportunities arise.

The following general suggestions can help you keep ICPS alive in your classroom after the lessons are over:

1. Apply ICPS teaching to the stories you read or reread in class.
   At any point, ask children if they remember what happens next, or, for a new story, to guess what might happen next. Encourage children to draw the problem, characters' feelings, and how the problem was solved.

2. Have children draw their own problems, feelings, and solutions.
   In small groups or one-to-one, discuss these drawings.

3. Continue using puppets to help children role-play actual or hypothetical problems. As the puppets try to solve the problem, let them call on other children to help.

4. Repeat any lesson the children enjoyed or need more of. Whenever possible, let a child lead the activity.

Quiz yourself periodically on how ICPS is working for you as a teacher. Ask yourself whether you can think of a time when:

1. You recognized a problem with the children in your class
   a. by seeing but not hearing or asking
   b. by hearing but not seeing or asking
   c. by asking, but not seeing or hearing
   d. by two or all three of these ways

2. You made a child in your class feel
   a. happy
   b. sad
   c. angry
   d. afraid
   e. proud
   f. frustrated
   g. impatient
   h. worried
   i. relieved

3. A child in your class made you feel
   a. happy
   b. sad
   c. angry
   d. afraid
   e. proud
   f. frustrated
   g. impatient
   h. worried
   i. relieved

4. You learned something you didn't know about a child through ICPS dialoguing.

5. When a child or children were having a problem, you thought you knew what the problem was, but because you used dialoguing you found out it was actually something quite different.

You can also use the ICPS Teacher Self-Evaluation Checklist, which immediately follows, to help you evaluate your ability to apply ICPS principles in various interpersonal situations. Duplicate the checklist and monitor your use of the ICPS approach either daily or weekly. Over time, average your score within each category as you use the checklist. As your score decreases for Categories A through C, and increases for Category D, you are increasing your use of the ICPS approach.

ICPS TEACHER SELF-EVALUATION CHECKLIST

Date(s) _____

Rating Scale: 1   2   3   4   5
               Never   Sometimes   Always

(Today/this week) I found that with most children, I:

A. Demanded, commanded, belittled, punished   Score _____

Examples   Sit down!
You can't do that!
You know you shouldn't _____!
How many times have I told you _____!
Give it back!

B. Offered suggestions without explanation   Score _____

Examples   You can't go around hitting kids.
Why don't you ask him for it?
Children must learn to share.

C. Offered suggestions with explanation, including talk of feelings   Score _____

Examples   If you hit, you MIGHT lose a friend (get hurt).
If you grab, she won't let you play with her toys.
You shouldn't do that. It's not nice (FAIR).
You'll make him ANGRY if you do that.

D. Guided children to think of feelings, solutions, consequences   Score _____

Examples   What's the problem? What happened?
How do you think I (a child) feel(s) when _____?
What happened (MIGHT happen IF) _____?
What could you do so that would NOT happen?
Do you think that IS or is NOT a good idea?
(*If not a good idea:* Can you think of
a DIFFERENT way to _____?)

APPENDIX B

ICPS Dialoguing Reminders

Post the following pages in your classroom to help remind yourself and other teachers to use ICPS dialoguing when real problems arise during the day. As the dialogues in the lessons suggest, it is important to be flexible. The steps presented here are meant to serve only as a guideline.

Happy ICPSing!

CHILD-CHILD PROBLEMS

STEP 1: **Define the problem.**

What happened? What's the matter?
That will help me understand the problem better.

STEP 2: **Elicit feelings.**

How do you feel?
How does _____ feel?

STEP 3: **Elicit consequences.**

What happened when you did that?

STEP 4: **Elicit feelings about consequences.**

How did you feel when _____?
(*For example:* He took your toy/she hit you)

STEP 5: **Encourage the child to think of alternative solutions.**

Can you think of a DIFFERENT way to solve this problem
so _____?
(*For example:* You both won't be mad/she won't hit you)

STEP 6: **Encourage evaluation of the solution.**

Is that a good idea or NOT a good idea?
If a good idea: Go ahead and try that.
If not a good idea: Oh, you'll have to think of something
DIFFERENT.

STEP 7: **Praise the child's act of thinking.**

If the solution works: Oh, you thought of that all by yourself.
You're a good problem solver!
If the solution does not work: Oh, you'll have to think of
something DIFFERENT. I know you're a good thinker!

TEACHER-CHILD PROBLEMS

Can I talk to you AND to _____ at the SAME time?

Is that a good place to _____?

(*For example:* Draw/leave your food)

Can you think of a good place to _____?

Is this a good time to _____?

(*For example:* Talk to your neighbor/talk to me)

When IS a good time?

How do you think I feel when you _____?

(*For example:* Don't listen/throw food/interrupt me)

Can you think of something DIFFERENT to do until _____?

(*For example:* You can fingerpaint/I can get what you want/I can help you)

ICPS Word Concept Illustrations

Display the following illustrations on classroom walls or a bulletin board, or mount them on posterboard and use them as flash cards. They will help remind both teachers and children to use ICPS words during the day.

Is

This *is* a girl.

Not

This is a boy.

He is *not* a _____.

Or

You may have a _____ *or* a _____.

And

He is wearing
shoes *and* socks.

Some

Some of these are books.

All

All of these
are toys.

If-Then

If you have a key, *then* you can lock the door.

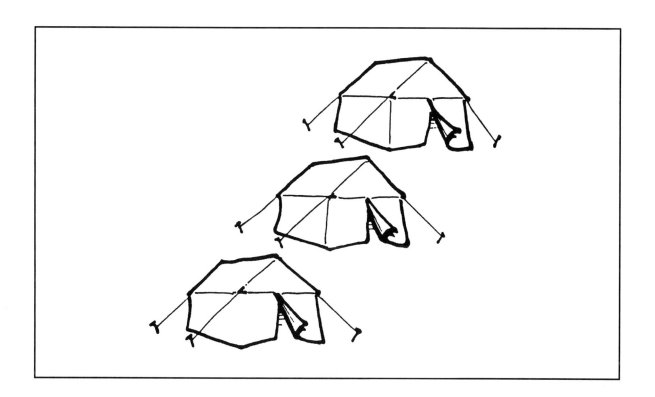

Same

All of the tents are the *same*.

Different

Each bow is *different*.

Before

Before you go to bed, close the window.

After

Father said,
"We will eat
after I cook."

Now

Mother said,
"Mop right *now!*"

Later

Mother said,
"Mop now,
play ball *later*."

Might

What *might* he do next?

Maybe

"*Maybe* we will have rain today," said Ken.

Why

"*Why* are you sad?" asked Mother.

Because

"I am sad *because* my cat is sick," said Kim.

APPENDIX D

Summary of ICPS Behavior Management Techniques

Experience suggests that, if teachers are sensitive to "difficult" behaviors and ready to accept and incorporate them and the child into the training process, the program moves smoothly and both teacher and children are able to enjoy it every step of the way. The following techniques, given as hints in the lessons, will help you manage these behaviors during ICPS lesson time.

SHY, NONRESPONSIVE BEHAVIORS

1. Encourage extra use of body movements, as in Lesson 9. If nonresponsiveness is extreme, guide the child by saying, "Let's shake our heads together" in answer to a yes-or-no question (for example, "Are you jumping?"). This technique helps the child move beyond complete passivity.

2. Offer one-word choices. For example, in response to a question such as "How do you feel when. . .?" offer "HAPPY or SAD?"; "SAD or ANGRY?"; and so forth. To a question such as "We are NOT doing the SAME thing as Tommy. We are doing something _____?" offer the choice, "SAME or DIFFERENT?" In this way, the child does not have to respond to an open-ended question or verbalize a whole sentence.

3. Encourage the child to draw feelings and problem situations. The child then does not have to express them verbally.

4. Let the child point in lessons where this is appropriate (for example, in Lesson 22, where illustrations are chosen). Again, the child is participating without having to speak.

5. Let the child respond through a puppet character. "Poppy the Pup" may express ideas, even though Keshia does not. After getting used to responding as the puppet, the child may begin responding, however slowly, as herself.

6. In the lessons devoted to problem-solving skills, avoid the temptation to offer solutions or consequences yourself. Many shy nonresponders will begin to offer their own ideas soon after they feel comfortable verbalizing.

7. Praise any level of response. When given the opportunity to respond and generous praise, most shy nonresponders blossom.

DISRUPTIVE OR OBSTINATE BEHAVIORS

1. After the ICPS word concepts SAME and DIFFERENT are introduced (Lessons 9 and 10), use them to bring a child who is disruptive or obstinate back into the group. You might say, for example, "Robert is fussing. The rest of us are jumping. Is Robert doing the SAME thing OR something DIFFERENT from the rest of us?" Using the concepts this way avoids a power play, which only propels the child to fight back or become more obstinate.

2. After feeling word lessons (for example, Lessons 17 and 18) have been conducted, ask the child how she is feeling. Let the group try to think of ways to help the child feel better. Using the Do You Like Game (Lesson 23) can also help. One child who was pouting was asked, "Do you like horses?" The child smiled and came right back to the lesson. If the child does not respond to such inquiries, do not push. Asking the child to join or leave the group may only cause a negative association with the lessons.

3. Be careful to distinguish disruptive or obstinate behavior from true upset. In addition, avoid taking so much time dealing with a disruptive or obstinate child that other group members become restless.

DOMINATING BEHAVIORS

1. A child who tells long, drawn-out stories can create a loss of interest in the rest of the group. Use the words DIFFERENT (Lessons 9 and 10) and NOW (Lesson 13) after they have been introduced. For example, you might say, "Dennis just had a turn. NOW someone DIFFERENT needs a turn." This technique helps the dominating child become more aware of others' needs.

2. If you think the child will not be upset, use the words NOT (Lesson 1) and FAIR (Lessons 40–42): "If Dennis has had a very, very long turn and Rashad has NOT had any turns, is that FAIR?" This technique is another way of keeping the dominating child in the lesson.

3. Realize that extremely verbal children often unintentionally dominate the group. Handle them with care, using the techniques already presented to avoid alienating them.

SILLY BEHAVIORS

1. Respond to children who intentionally give irrelevant or opposite answers, or who laugh hysterically or make faces or funny gestures, by saying quietly, "Oh, you're just teasing me" and continuing with the lesson. Negative reactions tend to perpetuate silly behavior.

2. Shy nonresponders may parrot others' responses; if so, they should not be pushed to provide another answer. However, if a child repeats others' responses in a silly manner just to gain attention, she may be told directly, "I know you can think of something DIFFERENT." This kind of attention helps the child learn.

3. If a child continues to be silly, you may simply ignore him. If he is also being disruptive or obstinate, you may also use the techniques listed earlier. When the child does respond normally, be sure to praise the new behavior. Silly behavior due to lack of ability to contribute often diminishes as children learn the concepts of the program.

ABOUT THE AUTHOR

Photograph by Nora Alba

Myrna B. Shure, a developmental psychologist, is a professor in the Department of Mental Health Sciences at Hahnemann University in Philadelphia. Her ICPS programs and her pioneering research with George Spivack have won three national awards. One of these, the Lela Rowland Prevention Award (1982), was from the National Mental Health Association. Two were from the American Psychological Association: the Division of Community Psychology's Distinguished Contribution Award (1984) and an award from the Task Force on Promotion, Prevention, and Intervention Alternatives in Psychology (1986). The task force chose ICPS as one of their nationwide model prevention programs.

Dr. Shure is the author or coauthor of four books and numerous book chapters and journal articles. Her new book for parents, *Raising a Thinking Child* (Henry Holt), helps young children learn to resolve everyday conflicts and get along with others. In addition to her writing and research, Dr. Shure also consults with the media on issues relating to social adjustment and interpersonal competence in our nation's youth.